Angelyn Spignesi

Starving Women
A Psychology of Anorexia Nervosa

Spring Publications, Inc.
Dallas, Texas

Printed in the United States of America by BookCrafters, Chelsea, Michigan, for Spring Publications, Inc., P. O. Box 222069, Dallas, Texas 75222

International distributors:
Spring/Postfach/8800 Thalwil/Switzerland; Japan Spring Sha, Inc./31, Shichiku-Momonomoto-Cho/Kitaku, Kyoto, 603 Japan; Element Books Ltd/The Old Brewery Tisbury Salisbury/Wiltshire SP3 6NH/England

Cover: Adapted from an anonymous fifteenth-century alchemical depiction of the red flowering out of the white body, Biblioteca Apostolica Vaticana, Cod. Pal. lat. 1066, f. 230v. and designed by Sven Doehner.

Library of Congress Cataloging in Publication Data

Spignesi, Angelyn.
    Starving women.

    Includes bibliographical references and index.
    1. Anorexia nervosa. 2. Women—Mental health.
3. Archetype (Psychology) 4. Mythology, Greek—Psychological aspects. 5. Feminism. I. Title.
RC552.A5S74   1983   616.85'2   83-20065
ISBN 0-88214-325-5

Acknowledgments

Chapters of this book have been published in *Journal of Obesity and Weight Regulation* as well as in *Sulfur*, a poetry journal.

The author wishes to thank Eileen Gregory for her careful and original copyediting, Mary Helen Gray for typesetting and production management, Marilyn Holt for typing, and Patricia McGarry for typing as well as indexing the manuscript.

The author is grateful to the following publishers for permission to reprint material in this volume:

   From *Essays on a Science of Mythology* by C. G. Jung and C. Kerenyi, Copyright 1949, © 1959, 1963 by Princeton University Press, by permission of Princeton University Press.

   From *The Golden Cage* by Hilde Bruch, Copyright © 1978 by the President and Fellows of Harvard College, by permission of Harvard University Press.

   From *Eating Disorders* by Hilde Bruch, Copyright © 1973 by Basic Books, Inc., by permission of Basic Books, Inc.

*For my mother
and her ocean*

Contents

Preface

Each psychology is a confession, and the worth of a
psychology for another person lies not in the places
where he can identify with it because it satisfies his
psychic needs, but where it provokes him to work
out his own psychology in response.

James Hillman, *Re-Visioning Psychology*

One night a while ago my colleagues and I were discussing
psychology on the corner of Routh and Hibernia Streets in
Dallas, Texas. We were delineating what we wanted to discuss
in our weekly talks, what psychological issues moved us. I men-
tioned that I was quite concerned that all we have left of
Freud's female hysterics and Jung's female psychopaths and
companions are Freudian and Jungian volumes of interpretation and theory. I was troubled that somehow the *substance* of
the woman's psyche had vanished, that I could not locate it in
all those volumes.

My colleagues did not understand my concern. The more
they were perplexed, the more anxious, even urgent, I became.
I left that evening outwardly calm but inwardly confused and
hurt. That year (1980) I finished the first third of this manuscript; the complete version was completed this year (1982).

These two years mark the hundredth anniversary of the treatment of Anna O. (Breuer's hysteric whom Freud "adopted")—she became ill in 1880 and was healed in 1882. Anna O. has been a background figure through much of my work on this manuscript, not only because I feel that anorexia is the modern offspring of hysteria but also because I regret that we never received an account of Anna's psychic exploration in her own words. Breuer alludes to her discovery of her own "talking cure," her active imagination and physical enactments while encountering her psychic demons, but we never meet the actual imaginal figures nor are we permitted to walk with her through the imaginal landscape which did usher in some of Freud's theory of the unconscious. In the same way, I am left wondering about Jung's patient/friend Sabina Spielrein—where is her volume on the death instinct? What happened to her attempts to articulate the domain of her intense psychic suffering?

So I offer this book as an invitation to all of us 'hysterics' to begin to write on our own from the psyche which is our own and inherently that of a woman. The female unconscious has been scrutinized, analyzed, and categorized by brilliant depth psychologists, yet each essentially has offered us this exploration seen, of course, from his own psyche. This book revolves around the theme of the woman's relation to the psychic underworld, to the imaginal figures and landscape underlying and permeating her bodily existence. It is time for women to enter the unfamiliar chasm of our own psychological terrain and to carry this up in aesthetic endeavor. It has been waiting long enough, emerging as symptom long enough, sending us to be 'cured' by external clinicians and physicians long enough. Time to find the monsters in our symptoms, witness their transformation to inner healer, and create from that.

A statement is needed on terminology. The book rests on the assumptions—from the works of Freud, Jung, and Hillman—that an underlying psychic realm permeates all everyday behaviors, thoughts, attitudes, values, emotions, sense-perceptions. Following Jung and Hillman, I use the terms "underworld" and "upperworld" in discussing this. Both terms represent perspectives we have, ways we see the world. When we are in an upperworld perspective, we view ourselves and the world as it literally exists—as objects in time and space which we can observe or even measure, the world as immediately and objectively present to our consciousness. In an underworld perspective, we see that everything material points back to or carries autonomous figures of the psyche which are collective, which cross generations, and which are not subject to time/space dimensions of everyday 'reality.' These figures often are dark, monstrous, and terrifying, and we can speak of encountering and learning to contain them as an underworld journey. Such a journey does not bypass the material givens. On the contrary, to enter the underworld, one must pay much attention to the specific phenomena 'above.' The underworld perspective does not abandon a sophistic or existential-phenomenological perspective to assume an idealistic, transcendental one. Instead, it allows and necessitates a sense of the interpenetration of the sensible world with the imaginal realm. Through this thin book on anorexia, I begin to explore the woman's underworld journey, and I am grateful to the wide body of feminist literature, some of which I cite in this work, presenting an overall context in which such an attempt finally can be valued culturally.

My intent here is to step gracefully into the psyche of the anorexic/bulimic in full openness to and respect for its substance and to tell the story from within the recesses of this psyche. The chapters revolve circularly, each one allowing us to drop deeper into the folds of the anorexic's psyche. In the last chapter, we are completely within her psyche. So we find that the language of this book changes slowly, and by the last chapter the images take over, speak for themselves.

One last note: though the book concerns itself with literal anorexics/bulimics, I take them to be the carrier of the *starving woman in every person*, the female starving to be nourished by the underworld from which she has been cut off for centuries.

The structure of the book begins with 'data' from literal anorexics and circulates this material while going deeper into psyche until we arrive at the figure of the starving woman who has a place for every woman.

West Hartford, CT.
May 20, 1982

Chapter I
Mother and Oppositionalism

Feminists today see the separation of the world of the Father from that of the Mother as the very foundation of Western culture and modern civilization. One could read the current feminist movement in terms of an attempt to deliver Mother from the literal kitchen. Over and over we read accounts by modern women of how the female has been stuck on earth while the heights of intellectual soaring as well as the depths of fiery, libidinal escapades have been lost to her or allocated to deviants of her gender.

Feminists see that Mother has been confined within the home from which we come: nature, food, soil. Women are bound to human life and love: bearing, consoling, reproducing, sheltering, succoring, sustaining life. Meanwhile men, at ease roaming through the night, become companions of the deathly nightworld. Men are given the right to disconnect the human from the vital material of life: wounding, butchering, raping, driving, preaching us out of life, elevating us above it, studying, revering, analyzing death and mysterious realms like the soul. The feminist rage at these dichotomies signifies new movement, a new consciousness entering into the culture.

For all the journeying into psyche and instinct, depth psychologists have not done much to see through the feminist issues—that is, to explore the imaginal location of the mytheme reflecting the opposition between Mother and Father, and Mother's mounting rage over it. If anything, they (particularly Freud) have perpetuated the separation between Mother and Father and all it represents: emotional histrionics versus psychological systematization, home versus civilization, the care of infants versus world distribution of psychic energy.[1] I am not concerned here with whether Freud's work is amenable to a feminist perspective; others have done that.[2] I am concerned that consistently within his imaginal landscape the female figure is identified exclusively with the literal earthly home, with aspects of emotion and nurturance. In *Civilization and Its Discontents*, Freud summons forth Eros, originally identified with the woman, to save us from the mess of the civilization, the instinct of Thanatos, identified with the man.[3] Thanatos and Father penetrate and soar up; women are left at home, on earth, extending with the breadth of an ample bosom the fullness of Eros in order to counteract the rampant destruction of the Father. Vertical versus horizontal, Father versus Mother, Thanatos versus Eros: what this view constellates is opposition, domination, conquest.

But to call for an upsurge of the 'other side'—that is, of emotion, fertility, and earthly fruition, commonly located in the female, the black, the poet, and the madman—is not tenable since that confines us to the classic position, opposite the Big Boys. Even an uprising of the underdog will not work to extricate us from stultifying identifications; it would only change which opposing side is on top. Glorifying Female and Womb is not the answer.

All this allows me to ask just this: Is the problem one of destroying the Father, or is it that Father has dominated so long to the exclusion of other elements? Is the incredible violation and destruction of a planet, evident everywhere, an aspect of the Father per se or the result of the narrow domination of only one psychic dominant, one way-of-seeing?

This has led me to question whether the task is to make Mother Queen (or King) or to rid ourselves of opposition altogether. To let the female finally appear—in full physical and psychological expression[4]—we no longer have to imagine her as opposite. We are beginning to find that the more we define female as high, superior, dominating, the more we constellate the destruction of everything known as female.[5] Attempts to become equal to or to imitate the male will be only a phase in the recovery of an inherent femininity (Rilke saw this years ago).[6] Modern feminist leaders already have showed the implicit problems and dangers for women to subscribe to such homogeneous concepts as androgyny and humanism.[7] The issue is not merging, diluting, or even dialectics. It is, rather, refusing to see in opposites, instead taking Mother and Father as continually in motion, without hierarchy, within one another yet with precise distinction and differentiation.

This desire to avoid fixed dichotomies returns us to depth psychology, particularly recent work by James Hillman, who warns of the dangers of oppositionalism for the study of psychic depths. He acknowledges the hold such an orientation has on our consciousness, in apologia for his own dichotomous view[8] as he opposes the material upperworld and psychic underworld.[9] Using differentiations of Great Goddess Gaia (Ge), he claims that our consciousness has been focused too long on 'above': on the literal, material world (Ge–Demeter) and the order (Themis) of that earth (Ge–Themis). He contrasts this realm with the chthonic realm of Hades, the underworld (Chthon), the land of psychic figures, the stuff of dream life, ambiguous vistas, and mysterious desires.

Hillman is somewhat able to move out of his own oppositions with a fine section on the convertibility of emotion and psychic shade in his discussion of Dionysus/Hades. But Mother is still left stranded—up there, tied to kitchen or the rule of fertility, divorced from, and even a barrier to, psychological journeying through the kingdom of Hades.[10]

Nonetheless, Hillman's work did stir my imagination on the problem with Mother. It expresses the problem itself: Mother is so stuck in material that this able depth psychologist cannot pry her loose. In one of his earlier works, Hillman sees the inherent difficulties of postulating hierarchical models with distinct polarities. He remarks that models of the psyche usually come packaged in three layers, from Plato's aspects of the soul to Freud's id–ego–superego, and suggests we abandon such models since they necessitate the inferiority of a 'lower' position.[11] In a sense he foresees a later difficulty with his Demeter–Ge–Chthon discussion, in which, since he takes his stand with Hades, the inferiority moves to the top layer, home to Mother. Yet, as a proponent of polycentricity, circulation, and rotation, he urges us to see through his own model. Hillman himself reminds us not to take Hillman literally. This becomes our challenge: to see through his Demeter–Ge–Chthon motif, to find where and who Mother is in the underworld and where the place of death is in the kitchen.

In full sight of and respect for the stance of Mother as well as that of the underworld, I would like to examine this transition from the material to the psychical point of view and vice versa, to investigate convertibilities between upperworld concretism and underworld configuration. Where is the place of Mother? Who is she psychologically, and what does she want?

Hillman's statement itself on Mother's domination seen in our materialism, naturalism, personalism, and emotionalism reminds us that psychic figures cast egos and determine dayworld situations as they work themselves out.[12] Perhaps *they* have given us these demanding earthly manifestations of Mother; perhaps our materialism indicates that we have not done Mother justice (as feminists imply) by not having seen her in her rightful psychic place. Perhaps it is not that she represents a monotheistic, engulfing, literalizing perspective but that we have not contained her psychic form, have not given aspects of her their due respect. The Themis of Ge, which Hillman discusses in terms of upperworld morality, pertains to underworld, too: there are 'moral' implications to finding the rightful place of Mother in the underworld. Until we do discover it, we will probably remain oppressed by dayworld concretisms which seem to war against the psychic realm.

The Anorexic and Methodology

This necessity that the psychic place of Mother be uncovered leads me to wonder: Who is struggling for Mother today? Who has Mother chosen to enact her relation with Hades, with the underworld, the realm from which she has been excluded? I pause: my glance is held by the spectacle of the anorexic. Here we have a woman who explicitly enacts a war against aspects traditionally binding the female to the material earth—food, body, reproduction.

We are not the first to look upon this emaciated figure. For one hundred years she has beguiled, evaded, and aggravated the medical and psychiatric professions. Physicians and clinicians have viewed her from physiological, pediatric, psychoanalytic, phenomenological, developmental, and behavioristic frameworks. They have argued back and forth about whether she deserves her own diagnostic category, whether she represents a separate "psychiatric entity" or a syndrome common to other disorders.[13] They have searched for the causes of her voluntary starvation and have proposed numerous cures.

For one hundred years, medical and psychological experts have been attempting to put this female skeleton back into shape. Thoma comments that the history of anorexia nervosa itself has mirrored the changing modes of medicine and psychology.[14] We see the anorexic go through isolation cures and heat treatments in the late nineteenth century; physiological models in the early twentieth; to psychoanalytical interpretations in the decades of the forties and fifties; followed by behavioral reinforcement and electroshock therapy in the sixties; and by frontal leucotomies, tubefeeding, and hospital isolation in the seventies.[15] All reports, no matter what orientation, follow the basic medical outline: Identity–Etiology–Treatment.

So our first methodological announcement is that such studies are upperworld classifications. That is, they are made by doctors who are standing in the dayworld perspective and looking diagnostically upon the anorexic patient. Their upperworld stance is demonstrated by the fact that they work with what they see externally and materially (for example, her size, weight, behavior) as well as by the attempt to contain such observations in empirical, personalistic, and developmental formats.

The second methodological decision is not to ignore or bracket such studies, in spite of our claim of being concerned primarily with the psychic underworld. The meticulous observations of one hundred years offer us glimpses from many perspectives. Though our primary focus will be from below, we must remember that there is one figure here; the simultaneity of underworld with daily world necessitates a respect for upperworld findings too. The anorexic herself, described consistently throughout the century as perfectionist, meticulous, scholarly, would not want it any other way.

One consequence of this approach is that we will not use the doctors' texts as attestations of historical fact or accumulated authority—we need not take the clinical and medical interpretations as positivistic truths about the anorexic. Nor will we pretend that the findings of this decade are more important or truthful or medically correct than those of the thirties and forties. Each study contributes a certain upperworld, cultural perspective; all will be helpful, and none is 'outdated.'

These upperworld perspectives will not be eliminated; neither will they be bracketed, delegated to a separate chapter or section. Scientific and medical findings are easy scapegoats of archetypal psychology.[16] Such a dialectical maneuver is not necessary since we remember "that the opposite is already present"[17] in any perspective. The doctors may be standing in the dayworld and speaking a language other than that of the psyche, yet they are careful watchers. We can use what they have seen because, though we are less interested in correct interpretation than in the underlying guiding presence, the two—dayworld and psyche—are not alien or opposite. Within one perspective we can see the other. Through both, we find her.

Researchers have been strongly drawn to this figure; they have eyed her carefully. The voluminous amount of research done on a relative paucity of cases illustrates how vividly the anorexic has caught the imagination.[18] Researchers have been attached to her, perhaps even enamored. The presences moving through her pathology have their counterparts speaking through the observations and thoughts of the scientists and psychiatrists. The same archetype appears in symptom as well as thoughts about the symptom; the Gods of this disease will be reflected in its pathos as well as in its logos.[19]

Throughout this exploration we will remember that our basic thrust is to find the imaginal location of a certain mytheme in our culture pertaining to the opposition of Mother and Father. The assumption here, thoroughly discussed elsewhere,[20] is that psychic territory has its own configurations and that they lead us. If we follow these closely, open ourselves up to their transitions from underworld to upperworld, we will not be led astray. We will flow with the material because we have given ourselves over to the anorexic patient as guide. This does not mean becoming the anorexic or identifying with her afflictions but rather following her pathology to its root metaphors and back again to its worldly sufferings.

Cadaverous Female

The creases in the skin around the mouth and lips are so deep that they look like hags. Every curve has disappeared, the stomach is hollow, the limbs like sticks. Even when the patient stands with her legs together, there is a yawning gap between her thighs.[21]

This is a modern description of the anorexic. She always has appeared, first and foremost, as a starving woman.[22] A woman close to death, she brings us the deathly woman. Her ability to carry death so vividly while still alive fascinated one doctor as early as 1689, who commented that his patient was "like a skeleton only clad with skin."[23]

Faced with this female skeleton, the doctors are stunned. Gull and Lasegue—the two pioneers in the description of anorexia nervosa one hundred years ago—were amazed and alarmed by a disease which would cause a once plump and jovial young lady to starve herself to death.[24] In 1909 Dubois comments, "They do not know why they do not eat; as a rule they do not even think that they are sick. All feminine coquetry has disappeared in them, and they admit, without being in any degree impressed by it, their paleness and the fact they have wasted away to skeletons."[25]

Observing this cadaverous lady, the doctors report her jutting bones, cracked, dry, and scaly skin, brittle and lifeless hair and nails, yellow and loose teeth. Her extremities are blue and cold, her body temperature falls very low, and menstruation ceases altogether. Her skin increasingly appears pallid with a grayish tinge and becomes inelastic. Since the 1880s, her low heartbeat and generally decreased basal metabolic rate have seemed to the medical profession to be in sharp contrast to her hyperactivity, her continual, compulsive, repetitious behaviors. Also perplexing to physicians has been her indifference to her closeness to death, indeed her complacency toward and enjoyment of it.

The doctors note her tremendous hostility and basically antagonistic attitude toward all those around her, particularly those who would attempt to restore or cure her. All investigators and therapists remark on the anorexic's transformation from a compliant, conscientious, ambitious, meticulous, and highly principled young lady into the other personality ushered in with the disease, which is antagonistic, intolerant, authoritarian, and hyperactive to a degree excessive for her extreme emaciation.[26]

We see, then, not the dying female but a woman very much alive and active who brings us death.[27] First, she frightens us. This is not the female we expect. Gone are the full breasts, gentle curves, engaging smile, sensual enticement, and warmth. Binswanger's case study of Ellen West (whom modern psychologists recognize as an anorexic) describes the gradual change in the patient's expression to one which is "old and haggard."[28] He comments that this reflects her "existential death, the 'being-a-corpse among people'" and her perpetual desire to die.[29] He states that this was not a desire for a literal end to things as much as a longing for a union with the ethereal realm beyond the world, a "being-beyond-the-world" relating to a perception of "the pure essence of the world" which for her becomes separate from the world of biological needs.[30] This ethereal, nonresisting realm becomes more and more desirable to her in contrast with everyday material and earthly life, which she metaphorically describes in terms of a "prison": the curse of the stifling existence of a "blind earthworm."[31]

The anorexic alarms us, yet she also intrigues us. We are drawn to this "active struggle against [her] normal biological needs"[32] as much as we want to end it. She beckons us with her deathly airs as much as she repels us; she alarms us as she moves us. In response we want to set her straight. Consider the urgency with which the doctors attempt to return her to her "rightful" nature:

> Primary anorexia brings emotional development to a halt, and stops both physical and psychological maturation at an important stage. This is itself an urgent reason for insisting that a patient regains weight steadily, and enters the hospital if she fails to do so. It is essential that the therapist makes this understood by the patient and her relatives from the outset. In most cases, the weight target is around 90% of the ideal weight for the patient's age, sex, and height. This target should be agreed upon with the patient as soon as possible.[33]

Let us see how this deathly female of antagonism and self-destruction looks from an underworld perspective. Here we have a tight, shriveled skeletal frame which could well fit in the box of death. Like the skeletons stripped of flesh by Cerberus, she shows us the essential structure on which her life has been patterned. She brings us the essence of female life from a realm other than life. She shows those of us who believe we are living horizontally, within the confines of the living only, that there is death here too. Through her we see that even in what we consider traditional aspects of vitality and nurturance—feminine body, feminine nature—there is death. She evokes memories of shades, ghosts, and hags and carries up to us the world of shade, specifically the shade of the female.

With this woman of death we are forced to ask: Who or what dies? She who dies is the compliant Father's daughter, the yes-woman, the obedient nice-young-lady. What dies are the curves of a female body, the emotions of tenderness and warmth, as well as the fertility brought by the menstrual cycles. Psychologically, she lives below the world of emotion and sensuality.

From above, physicians and clinicians have seen this pathology in an antithetical relation to 'normal' emotional and sexual development. As early as 1873, Lasegue saw voluntary inanition in terms of a concealment or rejection of some emotion.[34] Rahman et al. describe how the disorder serves to kill the "gross or physical" in the female and allows her to avoid a natural emotional life and mature sexuality.[35] Binswanger describes Ellen West's view that her relentless starvation was opposed to a life of human love and to the role of a "wife": "I am choking in this petty, commonplace life."[36] He notes, "One has less the impression that she suffers under a genuine depressive affect than that she feels herself physically empty and dead, completely hollow, and suffers precisely from the fact that she cannot achieve any affect." Ellen herself describes her condition: "I am in Siberia; my heart is icebound, all around me is solitude and cold."[37]

Thoma, using Anna Freud's work on "asceticism at puberty," speaks of the anorexic's antagonism to the instinctual which gets resolved through "complete neutrality and an attempt to go beyond all human feelings."[38] He cites a case, Henrietta A., whose etiology relates to blushing. She began blushing whenever a male looked at her or when anything connected to love was brought up. Eventually, she found that fasting would subdue her fear of blushing, and with increased weight loss the blushing did disappear. Hence he sees the syndrome as a "sexual defense" and "drive disturbance."[39]

So anorexia is antithetical to the first flush of new love; the anorexic resides below our blushing, apart from mature emotion and sexuality. The doctors of the upperworld interpret this stance in terms of absence: negatives and frigidity. For example, a well-established definition of the syndrome by the specialist Hilde Bruch includes the following three aspects: (1) disturbance of body image—absence of concern with emaciation and defense of her appearance as regular; (2) loss of ability to perceive and identify bodily signals—absence of sexual feelings, inability to identify her emotions; (3) sense of ineffectiveness—negativism and defiance with which she wards off personal contact or treatment; her hostile, solitary, rigid nature.[40]

The doctors claim that her frigidity appears through her literal body, her emotional pattern, as well as her sexual response, in terms of absence: no body, cold body, absent emotion, asexuality. Certainly she shows us that she comes from a place beyond personal entanglement and passionate sexuality. From an underworld perspective we would not try to bring her back to life or warm her up but instead would ask what kind of body she lives within. What sort of connections do bind her? Where is the place of blood and heart in her cold connections? Hillman suggests meeting the cold at its own level in an underworld perspective instead of trying to heat it from above. It is as though in the following passage he could be speaking of what the anorexic is so visibly enacting:

> Here is a soul figure who is neither flighty, nor sensuously rippling, nor brooding moods and emotions. Instead the glitter of ice reflects perfection; nothing but crystallized insights and sharp-edged truths are good enough. Desire for absolutism in perfection. The ice-maiden is a terrible taskmaster, frigid and unresponsive; but since her region is on the map of psychic geography, polar coldness is also a place one can be. Therefore the urge to warm the cold and melt the ice (oppositionalism again) reflects a

therapeutic effort that has not been able to meet the ice at its own level. The curative urge conceals the fear of the Ninth Circle, of going all the way down to those depths that are so quickly and surely called psychotic.[41]

This allows us to see that perhaps here we have a soul figure living in the house of death, a Persephone who brings the realm of the dead into waking life. Instead of attempting to follow the lady into soul and to see her coldness in terms of its ancient connection to the soul,[42] since 1874 with Gull and his hot packs doctors have been trying to poke, pry, and even, with electroshock, fry her out of her frigid nature.[43] The fact that she has been seen for a century in terms of negatives, absence, and loss indicates more than anything else the culture's neglect of death[44] and the failure to recognize the relation of the female to death.

Yet the anorexic continues to announce bodily the presence of death in life, the psychic aspect within our materialism. Our rejection of this demonstrates our upperworld preference for earthly life and love and the female's connection with these, as well as our bias against seeing her as messenger from a cold realm of inhuman essence. Our procedures to warm, stimulate, and fill her out again speak our urgent attempt to regain natural footing when confronted with a presence of death.

Chapter II
Female of Borders

In the last century the hysteric carried Freud to psyche; the anorexic may be our twentieth-century carrier. We will not analyze her or translate her message into upperworld languages. Instead we ask: If we do meet her on her own level, what do we find? Instead of meeting starvation, we find the experience of being well-fed, even fat. Over and over the anorexic announces to the doctors that she is not too thin. When she looks upon her skeletal shape, she 'sees' fat. The doctors have noted this claim to be too fat and have interpreted it as a denial and distortion of her body image.[1] The upperworld sees it as manifesting the patient's distorted thinking and as an absence of emotional investment in her emaciation. Yet from the underworld where her image of the body, her imaginal body, becomes the focus, she is fat.

What is publicly seen as emaciation, from an imaginal perspective is seen as fat. Her fat is hidden. Hers is an invisible fullness. Again she brings us to the realm beneath our naturalistic perspective, to the underworld, realm of Hades. The wealth of Hades is not substantial; we cannot touch or trade it.[2] Likewise the anorexic's body and blubber are insubstantial. We find her fat, her invisible presence, through what looks from above as loss, emptiness, nothingness.

This lacuna offers us psychic awareness of that which is 'lacking.' We look at the skeletal figure and more than ever are presented with that which completes the obvious lack: an image of the breasts and hips of the mature female. The anorexic lives within this psychic (not literal) awareness of the female. This allows us to see how the reflection of the female, psychic awareness of her, is lacking in our culture, which relies too simplemindedly on the pin-up model. Doctors will not abandon their naturalistic view of the female, so they must claim that this underworld view is a lie, distortion, deception.

Indeed, this lady of invisible presence has baffled doctors with her duplicity. One modern researcher discusses her deception of the family as well as of the hospital. All along the family believes the anorexic is eating huge amounts of food; it comes as a surprise when the doctor informs them of their daughter's starvation.[3] She so lives in a body of fat that those closest to her begin to see her according to this imagistic perspective.

Since she is already fat, at all costs and with much duplicity she must avoid forced feeding by the doctors. In the hospital she gives food to other patients, stuffs it in pillowcases and handkerchiefs, throws it out the window, or vomits in secret. She sews weights into her clothing to boost the scales to a satisfactory margin so she can return home.[4] Meyer and Weinroth observe that:

> Tricks, concealments, and artifices are employed in profusion by these frail, angel-faced gamins, who, testing and teasing, appear to be quite oblivious of the grave stakes with which they are toying. . . . For, in addition to the clinging importunities of the patient and her frequent mischievous manipulations, the physician has to deal as well with anxious relatives who view with increasing alarm the physical deterioration and weight loss of an individual who may be a source of guilt and an object of hostility.[5]

She tricks us, becomes trickster to us. She appears to us as trickster also in the sense that we never see her as entirely male or female. Her asexual appearance has captured the medical imagination as did her asexual appetite. We have to look twice when she appears: female without curves, male with long hair? Researchers comment on her third-sex attributes—that she steps outside of each gender. Bruch discusses the anorexic's early fantasies of being a prince or page boy and her eventual desire to become neither male nor female.[6] Binswanger describes Ellen West's early boyish games and later gender ambiguity, as well as Janet's anorexic case Nadia, who wanted to be neither sex.[7]

Theander included in his major questionnaire on anorexia an item inquiring about the patient's desire to have been a boy, and this obtained negative results.[8] Thoma states that Henrietta A.'s "narcissistic self-sufficiency and amazon-like autarchy" indicate her fear of the implications of the adult female role (that is, passivity and receptivity).[9] He adds, "The identification, however, is not exaggeratedly masculine; it would be better to say that a narcissistic, sexless existence is seen as providing a refuge from feminine, genital sexuality."[10] And more: she is "neuter, wanting to keep to a golden middle path, thus neither boy nor girl."[11] The anorexic is one who has stepped out of conventional gender.

Though physiological models were abandoned in 1940 when anorexia was found to be unrelated to the anterior pituitary dysfunction of Simmond's disease,[12] recent physiological findings testify to the scientist's fantasy of her as not quite female. Russell discusses recent laboratory investigations confirming that there is a failure in the output of gonadotrophins and estrogens in the anorexic even before she receives treatment, and refeeding does not lead to a complete recovery of hormones. He suggests that the gonadal failure itself might contribute to the abnormal and deficient sexual interest.[13] The primacy of gonadal and ovarian failure also is noted by Rahman et al., who found that endocrinological disturbance preceded the loss of weight for eight of their twelve patients. They also report the subnormal ovarian function after recovery.[14]

So scientists in the upperworld question the female attributes of the anorexic, wonder if she is fully female. They report her as a deficient female, yet not entirely male either; they remain perplexed, feel tricked. Again her refusal to be bound by literal and naturalistic categories bothers us. She refuses to be bound by categories exclusively equating woman with domestic hearth, receptivity, and nurturance. She defies identification by traditional gender. This, then, is the way that she comes to us, like other messages from the underworld, with duplicity and ambiguity.[15] She is not completely one thing, always suggesting an opposite; she remains in-between, homeless, back and forth —male and female, hyperactive and dead, frigid and fat, starving and well-fed, unemotional yet antagonistic, disciplined and autonomous yet dependent and frail.

Strange mystery lady of the borders... you are difficult to live with, you shake us, make us groundless. Gone are the traditional and useful guides to what is feminine. Your doctors urgently try to carry or translate you back to conventional, natural existence. Your duplicity and borderline nature unnerve us, bring about a change in us. Wherever we grasp, you disappear; whatever we categorize, you modify.

Whenever the doctors think they have the correct model, the interpretation which will cure it all, the anorexic offers another side which starts the diagnostic procedures all over again. Sooner or later we will see that what looks like paradox or duplicity to the upperworld is not only where the right way went haywire (for example, she distorts body image) but also where another story is unfolding (for example, she sees her emaciation as fat). Hence the duplicity of this enigmatic and rueful lady also allows her to serve as psychopompos. We see we have to go to soul to deepen and confirm her riddle instead of clarifying or eradicating it from above.[16] In her "double participation"[17] she makes us see the reality of many sides at once and refuses to become locked in any literal position.

As inhabitant of borderlines she can serve the double nature of upper- and underworld perspectives and perhaps initiate us into the underworld. Does this "lady of borders" have a ritual for such an initiation? Researchers have paid much attention to her bizarre and ritualistic behaviors; perhaps now we can see them in terms of their psychic significance.

Ritual Sacrifice of Food and Body

As this paradoxical lady reflects death within earthly life, she also carries a message about psychic nourishment. There is ritual in her non-participation in the conventional consumption of food. She develops concoctions on which she nourishes herself day after day. She lives on tidbits smothered with spices or salts prepared for certain meals which she prefers to eat alone instead of with the family. Attempts to make her eat dishes other than her prescribed ones are met with relentless hostility. Lettuce with mustard, half a bottle of lemonade and a lollipop, a tablespoon of ice cream, coleslaw and ketchup are recorded as typical feasts. She will be fiercely concerned over the quality of the food she chooses to eat: ice cream of a particular consistency, a vegetable cooked for so many minutes, coleslaw of a particular sweetness.

A scavenger, she rummages through pans or the refrigerator for scraps. Researchers tell us it is difficult, if not impossible, to find out when she eats or what. She eats in secret. She hides her food, eats alone, often standing up or moving. Her quantities of food are carefully measured out, calories and carbohydrates recorded or memorized. Caught in the act of eating, she is ashamed.[18]

Food for her is "alive" and potentially poisonous or dangerous.[19] A common cycle of anorexia now called bulimia is binge-starve or binge-vomit-starve. What distinguishes anorexia and bulimia from obesity and other food problems is the eat-purge cycle.[20] If the anorexic indulges in binge eating, she becomes panicked at the thought of the particles of food remaining within her. Since she perceives this food as alive and harmful to her being, she prepares to purge herself by vomiting or extreme starvation. The vomiting itself turns into an individualized ritual. It necessitates a special lavatory and a particular induction method, for example, a soft object to release the throat's gag mechanism. She must wait a certain number of minutes after the last portion of food is consumed: the food must be got rid of at all costs. Her panic at not obtaining enough of a specific food for a binge or a private place for vomiting demands that all other activities be put aside until the ritual is completed.[21]

This cycle has been documented in the literature for a century. In 1873 Lasegue remarks on the specificity of the anorexic's diet: how she would repetitively choose a particular "vegetable or viand" with many spices. He called this her "capricious restrictions."[22] Twenty years later Lloyd describes an anorexic case accompanied by severe vomiting: "The violent motor agitation, with constant vomiting and the eructation, gave the patient an extraordinary and ghastly appearance."[23] He notes that the presence of vomiting introduced an "element of danger" which had not been present in Lasegue and Gull's earlier cases.[24] It is as if our figure tries to return to the material world only to be compelled rapidly back to a starving body, to the realm of the dead.

Meyer and Weinroth speak of the obsessive nature of this cycle. They report how patients distinguish between the "good" anorexic phase and the "animalic" bulimic one. They describe how the anorexic continually alternates between "cannibalistic aggression and self-sacrifice, devouring greed and saintliness"[25] (another ambiguity). Eating becomes associated with sinfulness, starvation with saintliness. Starvation brings her to an "angelic," "ethereal" world.[26]

Bruch sees this ethereal elevation in terms of the anorexic's enjoyment of the vivid interior life accompanying the starvation: how the new hyperacuity and hypersensitivity to psychic experience convince her that she is on some "special" and "right road" to "purification."[27] A world of images is opened up. One of Bruch's patients, Elsa, who was "gifted as an artist and had done editing and writing," had obsessive "food thoughts" which came in "all shapes, sorts, and sizes." She says, "Sometimes I hear voices or feel things in my head, sometimes

I get frightening mental images."[28] Binswanger notes that Ellen West's ethereal existence was accompanied by creative bursts of imagery which she occasionally could contain in poetry. Yet the ethereal realm associated with starvation brought her imaginal presences beyond the human in other ways. Her "hunger" was accompanied by an intensified "longing," which she describes over and over, for the essential world beyond life. This realm beckons Ellen through the images of the "cold, grim Sea-King" with the "ardent love lust," the "Father (God) reigning behind the clouds," as well as the "great friend" or the "glorious woman, white asters in her dark hair, large eyes, dream-deep and gray."[29]

So starvation carries the anorexic to the mysteries of an otherworldly realm, allowing her to voyage away for a while from the world of material consumption to which she habitually returns in abandon and greed. How can we understand from an underworld perspective this ritual of the anorexic? We see that her starvation is associated with entering imaginal realms outside that of the natural and that for her food is a live, destructive presence which can harm. Perhaps we can grasp her bizarre habits by way of mimesis by finding a place where food is animate. What looks to the upperworld like self-starvation perhaps has a counterpart in ritual fasting. Important in ancient religious traditions, fasting and purification come down to us as rites of initiation signaling transformations between critical life phases as well as between life and death.

Primitive cultures have felt that certain foods convey evil influences into the body and that fasting delivers the body from such impurities. Thus fasting has served as a purificatory act and a ritual preparation to receive the realm beyond the natural. Likewise, we remember that Demeter was persuaded by Baubo to take food after a nine-day fast when her daughter Persephone was ravished by the lord of the dead. Specific purification rites and the eating and drinking of sacramental food, such as sacred cakes of sesame and the cyceon, became a part of the Eleusinian mysteries linking the human community to the presences of the afterlife.[30]

The initiates (mystai) of Eleusis killed an animal and fasted to be worthy to take Demeter's grief on themselves and prepare for the underworld mysteries.[31] The procession of mystai, who had fasted for nine days and drunk the cyceon, leads to the hierophant of the temple ("he who makes holy things appear").[32] In an elaborate ritual the hierophant calls for Persephone. As the sacred figure rises above the ground, the silent hierophant displays the mown ear of grain, allowing the initiates to partake of the sacred presence and the animation within it.[33]

Where the upperworld sees the anorexic's lack of consumption of 'real' food, the underworld perspective recognizes that her food is condiment, garbage, leftover, delicacy. She lives off of, gets substance from, what culturally is considered peripheral or waste. By making sacred through ritual the household scraps and fancies, perhaps the anorexic is evoking invisible presences, particularly the patroness of garbage, Hecate, Persephone's constant companion.[34]

Perhaps we can understand the food rituals of the anorexic as a sacrifice to Hecate: the food we discard as insubstantial brings her invisible substance. This is the food she places at the crossroads where Hecate dwells, and perhaps her ritual is how she evokes Hecate's understanding of the multiple senses beneath each concrete morsel. Each food particle has significance beyond literal digestion. She eats in secret: what feeds her is the secret quality of the food, its "alive" presence unknown to the upperworld which carries her to the realms of secrecy, the mysteries of the night.

What seems to the upperworld a diet of no-food or hidden food or extraneous food looks from below as the food of the psyche: the invisible psychic animation of food moves her, feeds her, drives her. Food carries psychic presence which is alive, harmful, destructive, death-dealing. Ellen West states:

> It [food] so fills up my brain that I have no more room for other thoughts; I can concentrate neither on working nor on reading. Usually the end is that I run out into the street. *I run away from the bread in my cupboard* [E. W.'S EMPHASIS] and wander aimlessly about. Or I take a laxative.[35]

Indeed, the anorexic tells the doctors that images of food surround, beckon, agitate, torment her. Food moves her psychically; it brings her shame and revulsion; it matters to the psyche.[36] She runs from its destructive nature as she is beckoned by it. This obsession with food takes many forms: she feels compelled to search for food, buy food, cook food, serve food to others continually.[37]

Dally and Gomez state that a piece of toast is seen by her as an entire loaf of bread, so taking one bite petrifies her.[38] Food carries some demon for her which we cannot see. Bruch describes how the anorexic complains of feeling "full" after a few bites of food or few drops of liquid. Bruch considers this a "phantom phenomenon" and goes on to describe how one of her patients claims that food gives her "weird ideas" such that the solid food remains intact even while in her "and that it becomes a part of me and thus has power over me." The patient continues: "It's not that I fear food as much as I fear the irrational feeling that somehow the food almost has the power over me that a person would—it is almost as if it (the food) could make me eat it."[39]

Hence, starving by eating only residuals takes the anorexic to imaginal realms outside the natural. Her consumption of food is perhaps an attempt to transform eating into a ritual for psyche. She eats, is fed and driven by what we cannot see. We ask: What feeds her? We see that she is fed by powerful images. She eats images. Images awake and feed her, move her to psyche and away from dayworld life. Perhaps she is attempting to release the psychic significance from concrete food; food has become a presence, a metaphor for what nourishes her, what moves her.

We see also that she attempts to release the psychic aspect from concrete body. Researchers continually refer to her exhibitionism and mirror gazing. She loves to show others her skeletal frame, as well as to stare at the mirror at her reflection (sometimes up to an hour).[40] Most doctors interpret this as childlike narcissism or egocentrism. From below we see it psychologically: she is fed by the image of the body in reflection. Her secret: the body, too (not only mind, consciousness, intellect), reflects; the body reflects psyche. Her body is fed by images, the true food of the psyche,[41] and this is reflected in body.

Modern psychologists understand her love of the reflected bodily image in terms of denial or condemnation of natural bodily instincts. They work at educating the anorexic to direct her focus on her own bodily signals and emotions.[42] This view confirms our observation that, for the anorexic, body is not the literal, vital, vegetative body of our biological instincts. Her body also reflects psyche; images fulfill her hunger as much or more than does literal food. It's time, she says, for the body to draw on psyche for nourishment.

The anorexic's syndrome, enacted bodily, shakes us out of one of our most rooted oppositions: body as instinct and emotion versus ephemeral intellect and reflection. She shows us a body driven by invisible, inhuman presences radiating from food which becomes alive and potent. No longer only vegetative, her subtle body reflects imaginal presence. We will see how her enactment demonstrates a desperate attempt to return female body to its psychic significance, serves to initiate the female out of her imprisonment within the naturalistic perspective binding her to inanimate matter and vegetation.

Deficient Ego: Polymorphous Child of Soul

From below we see the anorexic's bizarre behaviors in terms of primordial ritual allowing her to enter a reality outside the human and material. There she reflects back to us *our* psychic need for images that nourish. This figure of starvation turns us to our psychological starvation.

A description of primitive fasting allows us to understand the anorexic initiation into psychic presence. Macculloch reminds us: "In order to induce such dreams or to receive communications from supernatural or higher powers, fasting has been very commonly resorted to both among savages and among more advanced peoples, as well as in higher forms of religion." His many examples include the Plains Indians for whom fasting is used as a preparation for a lifetime guardian spirit (daimon) and also employed in the education of a medicine man. Further, fasting is ordinarily employed as a means of acquiring messages from figures in dreams.[43]

Bruch's rich descriptions in *The Golden Cage* assist us here. There is Elsa who has a continuous fear of being "not human" and a terror of "ceasing to exist." This patient feels "full of my mother—I feel she is in me—even if she isn't there." Another anorexic, Esther, discusses how she is unable to have one personality and effortlessly slips into a variety of female types. Zelda is another, accustomed to spending "many hours in the basement of her home, where she acted out lively fantasies and stories in which she had many friends. She was exceedingly secretive about this because she felt sure that such behavior would not be condoned." An extremely traumatic event for her was the removal of garden shrubs where she enacted her stories. College was desirable because it offered her a private room for such enactments without intrusion. Anorexia and a hectic increase in activities soon followed.[44]

Bruch discusses how the anorexic is confused about whether a sensation or impulse originates inside or comes from the outside; she feels no demarcation between self and others. Bruch further describes the anorexic as a blank or clean slate; that is, with each new person she develops different interests, a different personality. "They conceive of themselves as blanks who just go along with what the friend enjoys and wants to do. The idea that they have their own individuality to contribute to a friendship never occurs to them."[45]

These qualities relate to what researchers for decades have noted as the "deficiency of ego" of the anorexic. Gull in 1888 saw "perversions of the ego" as the cause of the course of the malady.[46] Crisp sees the entire syndrome in terms of conflicts arising from the assimilation by the patient of a delimited adult personality.[47] Bruch, citing Meng's work, also speaks of an "underlying deformation of the ego"; in all her papers her therapeutic approach is to develop autonomy and a sense of self. Bruch sees cure for anorexia in terms of success in teaching the patient to identify with and control her own functions. She adds that such therapeutic efforts are successful in conditions characterized by a "weak ego," "diffuse ego boundaries," or "narcissistic character." Selvini essentially agrees.[48]

This suggests the ability of the anorexic to become others imaginatively. Like that of a child, her reality is undivided; she can lose herself completely in the imaginal world of the other. Such open imaginative intercourse allows the anorexic to feed back and nurture the psychic presence ("personality") of the other. She continually reflects to others their guiding psychic figure. It is not that she lacks a unique "personality" but that her imaginal nature can take on many shapes and follow the multiple forms of the soul.[49]

In the medical fantasy of development, adult maturation, and ego differentiation, this quality of imaginal versatility implies that she is stunted and fixed at an early stage of development. Bruch discusses how (in terms of the Piagetian model) she is stuck at a "concrete, childish style of thinking." The anorexic's lack of self-assertion, abnormal considerateness, and deficient sense of autonomy convince Bruch that the patient is arrested at the pre-conceptual stage, the period of egocentricity characterized by concepts of magical effectiveness.[50] Bruch attributes this deficient development to a paucity of appropriate feedback responses; for example, the child's needs were responded to by the mother in contradictory or oversolicitous ways, leading to the patient's ineffective recognition of internal states, insufficiently differentiated responses, and general conceptual and perceptual deficiencies.[51]

From the underworld we see the "humanistic fallacy"[52] in such interpretations that reduce the polyvalence of psyche to human personality development. Within such a context the anorexic's multiple nature must be conceived as deficient, inferior, childish. Seen from above as regressed to a preconceptual stage with deficient ego boundaries and magical thinking, the anorexic seen from below appears as a child whose multiplicity well serves the underworld's polymorphous figures. We see here a "child of Hecate,"[53] and within the evocation of this child we return to the theme of the anorexic as a lady of borders, a guide of the underworld, who can move through a multiplicity of perspectives and ways of appearing.

This childlike quality makes even more obvious her borderline nature, her way of announcing to us that the opposite is always present. This nature of hers appears as contradictions in the upperworld literature, since it fails to see her as underworld child too. We have noted that she is seen in the literature as lacking a unique personality yet also is labeled narcissistic. Everywhere her high intelligence, overall creativity and achievements are noted, yet she is reported to be arrested at preconceptual levels of thought process. She is seen as childish yet described as never being literally childlike when an actual child.[54]

Ritual Blood Sacrifice

Such dilemmas and paradoxes of the anorexic become intelligible when regarded in the context of her role as psychopompos, carrier of soul. She recovers the psychic life in what is considered inanimate and returns death to what appears most alive and vital. To what seems unequivocally one way from the upperworld she lends an underworld viewpoint, and paradox results. Her rituals suggest to us that we can release the psychic potency from what is considered most material and earthy: food, body, instinct.

Likewise, she returns menstruation and pregnancy to the sacred world beyond and within that of the natural. Not only is hers a sacrifice of food and body to the Gods but one of blood also. She ceases menstruating as her reproduction becomes that of imaginal, rather than actual, pregnancy. We see that the skeletal figure must also return these female bodily functions to the invisible realm outside life, thus recovering for us their psychic significance.

Amenorrhea is considered by researchers to be correlated positively with a female's psychosexual immaturity, oral conflicts, and schizoid thinking or the incapacity to "differentiate between the real and the symbolic."[55] The suggestion from the doctors is that with the cessation of menses a woman is rejecting, denying, or fearing mature female sexuality.

In a thorough discussion of the psychological correlates of amenorrhea with focus on anorexia, Kelley et al. review the symbolic significance of the menstrual function. They remind us that symbolic connotations of menstruation have been with us since antiquity. Menstruation always has been associated with the province of Ge-Demeter: fertility, sexuality, aggressivity, emotionality.[56]

In an underworld perspective, instead of assuming that the anorexic is afraid of Demetrian functions we ask whether it might be that she knows this potency invisibly. Perhaps her life force, potency for life, is interior, held within, circulated internally. With her the functions of Demeter have gone to the invisible underworld: hers becomes an imaginative fertility. We remember that the pain and discomfort of menstruation tear us away from our dayworld contacts; with the splitting of our pelvis, the ground splits under us and we find ourselves hidden in isolation: lying in steaming bathtub, squirming under heating pad, crouching on pillowed couch. Menstruation returns us to the depths, opening our inner eye to the insights of the underworld as it shuts down our daily world contacts. For menstruation is the breakdown of life, the tearing apart of the life-bearing womb. As such it is a return to beginnings, to a time preceding life's construction; it takes the woman to the place of inhuman essence, to soul, to death.

The anorexic has no need of literal menstruation since already she lives in the realm of the inhuman to which it temporarily carries us. Her fertility is imaginative; she is fertile with invisible presences, pregnant with the images of psyche.

As messenger from the world of death, she was not chosen for material fertility but rather compelled to seek out the invisible pomegranate juices beneath all living things.

With the new symptom of amenorrhea, again we hear upperworld descriptions of the anorexic's difficulty with body imagery, poor definition of ego boundaries, deficient ego integration, and a concomitant faulty connection to her "aggressive and sexual impulses."[57] Certainly, she has moved out of the confines of a personal ego, has lost her differentiated ego to the polycentric psyche. What also goes is the visible materialization of Demetrian functions.[58] Like the doctors, Demeter would keep her naively eating concrete food and believing her body to be only literal. Yet now with the anorexic's vitality, her lifeforce, in the underworld, can we understand Demeter from a new angle? We still need to ask: Have we here Demeter in the underworld, Mother in the realm of the dead?

A review: staying close to this frigid lady, the anorexic, we found that her nourishment, her fertility, and her eroticism begin with imaginal food. She dreams of food, speaks of food, eyes it, hoards it, works it, and, as in sacrifice, serves it as sacred, showing us its invisible potency and its connection to invisible psychic realms.

What is for us one small cracker has for her the richness of an entire meal and allows her the ability to stay weightless, so she glides, flies as messenger of the soul. She reflects back to us both fleshy material greed and psychological starvation. She shows us how we have locked emotion and vitality with the flesh and hence suffocate. She shows us our earthly bias against death and our denial of the female's relation to those psychic realms. She shows us that we have not yet learned that our vitality, life-force, our wealth, lies beyond the human and natural world[59] and issues forth from invisible essences of the underworld. The mysteries of the soul: it is to them she calls us, with them she entices us.

Chapter III
Tyrant of Fat

From the perspective of upperworld investigators, one of the most intriguing aspects of this disorder is the lack of a hunger instinct or desire. The name of the disease itself incorporates just this (anorexia: absence of desire). Since the physicians and clinicians have seen "hunger drive" in direct proportion to the eating of substantial food, they have concluded that negative consumption means no desire for food.

However, recent research is concluding that "anorexia" is a misnomer.[1] The anorexic continually desires food, searches for it, cooks it, gives it to others, and generally lives off images of it. So some studies now discuss the compensatory relation between the hunger instinct and the imagination, that is, that hunger can be satisfied by *images* of food.[2]

Reimagined from a psychological perspective, the anorexic shows not that imagination is a pallid substitute for instinct but that the place of hunger is fulfilled, filled, by image. Anorexia seen from the underworld means "no desire" in the sense that desire is in the place of the invisible, the realm of the dead, or psyche: the anorexic desires the food of the psyche. Hence we need a truly psychic and imaginal therapy for her.

Thoma comments on the widespread attempt of the medical profession to regenerate the hunger drive of the anorexic. He suggests that these relentless attempts to determine what the disturbance is *not* contribute "nothing to the solution of the mystery of the vanishing nutritional drive, to which every other factor is subordinate, as Henri so rightly says. For it is precisely this problem which has remained unsolved."[3]

Absent nutritional drive: what drives her is not nutrition as we conventionally conceive it. In a former section we saw how food metaphorically opens her up to psychic presence. Now we can ask: Who drives her? In 1868, Gull spoke of the "morbid mental state" of these women. A girl once plump and compliant is transformed into a nasty and irritable skeleton. Gull attributed this change to a "morbid" psychogenic force with a direct neural energy effecting pathological changes.[4] A century later we must inquire: Who in the psyche forces such morbidity through these once compliant creatures?

On this question the anorexic has been clear: the inner tyrant, the dictator who dominates her. Meyer and Weinroth inform us: "An awareness of a cruel and ruthless inner force compelling the refusal of food and dictating every thought and act is in frequent evidence. Some patients spoke of 'something inside which makes me do it.'"[5]

Bruch describes the internal dictator who drives these females by regimentation and starvation to the brink of death:

> Others speak of feeling divided, as being a split person or two people. Most are reluctant to talk about this split. Sooner or later a remark about the other self slips out, whether it is 'a dictator who dominates me' or 'a ghost who surrounds me' or 'the little man who objects when I eat'. Usually this secret but powerful part of the self is experienced as a personification of everything they have tried to hide or deny as not approved by themselves and others. When they define this separate aspect, this different person always seems to be male.[6]

Bruch states that this figure, whether appearing as a little man, a shadow following them, or (in Sweden) as a troll, relates to their "inner compulsion," their sense of being a "hapless victim."[7]

This inner tyrant also pertains to what looks like the "willpower" in the anorexic. Bruch tells us that at first the vomiting and voluntary starvation allow the anorexic to think she is controlling her natural functions, but eventually this "gives way to the feeling of being helplessly in the grip of a demonic power that controls their life."[8]

Ellen West has much to say about the imaginal presence who drives her to starve. This "dread" of becoming fat follows her everywhere and images itself as an evil spirit who drives her against her plump, feminine "true nature":

> '*The entire world-picture is disarranged* [L. .B.'S ITALICS]. As if I were bewitched. An evil spirit accompanies me and embitters my joy in everything. He distorts everything beautiful, everything natural, everything simple, and makes a caricature out of it. He makes a caricature out of all life.'—'Something in me rebels against becoming fat. Rebels against becoming healthy, getting plump red cheeks, becoming a simple, robust woman, as corresponds to my true nature.... It drives me to despair that with all my big words I cannot get myself further. I am fighting against uncanny powers which are stronger than I. I cannot seize and grasp them....'[9]

This inner force which makes her dread fat and food dominates her existence so that her thoughts are exclusively on her body, eating, and laxatives. She describes the "morbid urge which rules her" as an enemy, a man "with a drawn sword" or an "armed man" who surrounds her and stops her whenever she tries to escape his domination. She adds that it is no good for the analyst to tell her this relates to "theatrical figments" and is "not real," because to her it is all "*very real*" (her emphasis).[10]

Since the upperworld stance understands such personification as inferior, archaic thinking, this information reinforces theories of the anorexic's regression to a childlike stage of development. From an underworld stance we ask: Who is this tyrant whose orders this young lady hears with an inner ear? Is he not an interior shadow, the invisible dark one who, rejected or denied in life, pulls her down to his realm of death? Perhaps now we can see this shade remaining behind and driving forth this female skeleton. It is Hades, through whom she sees that the wealth is beneath, that the nourishment of food is image, Hades who here in Ellen West's words makes "a caricature out of all life." Hades turns everything upside down: now what is invisible matters. Invisible presences resound; now her pregnancy is of images, and she remains with child.

The anorexic's experience brings us another side of this Hades figure. His driving her to starvation awakens the abundant imagery of food, the experience of how images feed. The tyrant directing her to starve brings her imagistically to food and fat. She sees food everywhere and sees herself as fat. When she is most driven, most starved, she sees herself as ripe, too voluptuous, and this repulses her. She finds that "along with the dread of getting fat goes an increased urge for sweets."[11] So the tyrant introduces her to the image of the fat one: to a metaphorical world of food and sensuality, to an imaginal realm which seduces her to orgiastic fulfillment, as much as that also repels her. The dictator is the one who keeps images of ugly, oily, fatty layers always in front of her: the opposite is always present. The dictator driving her to starve is also the fat one, the dionysian one. She is seized by the Dionysus within Hades,[12] oppressed by this presence. Her "absent nutritional drive," so perplexing to upperworld physicians, now appears as her being compelled by the master of underworld nourishment.

The psychological view of her "drive" in terms of the Hades/ Dionysus figure lets us make a place for what and who drives her, instead of having to work out the upperworld explanations of her drive: that is, for Thoma, drive disturbance; for Dally, regressive drive; for Crisp, reduction of sexual drive. What looks from an upperworld stance to be a problem of drive and instinct now becomes a study of the desire of invisible presences.

From the underworld stance we see she has the advantage of being close to a forceful figure of soul. Much potency is accessible to her. Yet, simultaneously, we see that there also is too much closeness here. Gripped by the Hades figure, without distance from or perspective toward him, she loses herself. The anorexic is oppressed by this figure, a victim to it; she is suffocating in her merging and overidentification with him. She has not become psychologically aware of this figure, of his shape, his voice, his desire, hence blindly lives out those qualities. She lacks a metaphorical view of him, so he returns in literalized form, seen in the upperworld as *her* tyrannical nature, *her* antagonism.[13] In this way he remains a symptom: the physicians and clinicians note her abnormal compulsivity, while he literally starves her to literal death.

The overidentification with this psychic tyrannical presence is demonstrated by Hazel: "You make out of your body your very own kingdom where you are the tyrant, the absolute dictator."[14] Another patient, Gertrude, states, "I thought it was just wonderful—that I was molding myself into that wonderful ascetic pure image. . . . I felt I had to do something I didn't want for a higher purpose. That took over my life. It all went haywire. I created a new image for myself and disciplined myself to a new way of life."[15] And Ellen West says, about her inner torment: "I long to be violated—and indeed I do violence to myself every hour."[16]

Selvini, Rahman et al., and others discuss this oppression of the anorexic. What begins as "willpower" eventually turns into a relentless power who controls her. This victimization of the anorexic appears in her exaggerated ambition, sense of duty, mental rigidity, and fixation in certain habits which assume a circular, obsessional character. It also results in the anorexic's assumption of a hostile and solitary stance: her refusal to cooperate with the therapist or any helper, her hypercritical judgments of her family, as well as her repetitive performance of secret gymnastics and isolated hyperactivity.[17]

The Tyrant's Drive
Hyperactivity, Bulimia, and Stealing

So the dictator who starves the anorexic also becomes her repetition compulsion. An aspect of her "compulsive nature" discussed in the literature is her "hyperactivity." Let's look at this phenomenon in detail. In 1873, Lasegue noticed that the patient felt more light and active than normal, was "able to pursue a fatiguing life in the world without perceiving the lassitude she would at other times have complained of."[18]

Gull (and much later Bruch) refer to the compulsive walking rituals, the emaciated creature relentlessly walking through all sorts of weather. Ushakov speaks of how this hyperactive behavior maintains the appearance of purposefulness. She cleans already clean floors, engages in physical exercise, helps with domestic work, insists on working with children while she herself is in the hospital.[19] As we have seen, this repetitious and compulsive activity generally pertains to food: she learns the calorific value of every morsel and spends long hours in the kitchen preparing food which she insists everyone but herself eat. She tries to take over the kitchen from her mother or force the mother to cook the same kind and quality of food daily. She repetitiously engages in strenuous exercise to insure a continual shedding of any absorbed calories.

This hyperactivity is associated, in the literature, with both bulimia and stealing. When the anorexic does consume actual food, she does not eat but rather gobbles as if taken over by a "grasping instinct."[20] She stuffs quantities and combinations of food into her mouth repetitively; once the gorging cycle begins, she has to complete it to the point of bursting. Not one cookie but the entire bag must be devoured in a frenzied manner. Her frantic consumption can drive her to a store at any hour to obtain and consume a quart of ice cream, potato chips, cupcakes.

This "grasping instinct" can be seen in her stealing, also. She seizes and hoards articles of food she could obtain easily by other means or sneaks money out of her mother's purse to buy food (though she never touches a penny of the father's money even when it is quite accessible).[21] She does this, too, in a kind of blind frenzy. We can see that her inward eye and ear which let in the tyrant have become closed through literalization of his desire to grasp.

The physicians and clinicians note that periods of frantic consumption and hyperactivity are accompanied by an overwhelming sense of emptiness. Bruch, Meng, Meyer and Weinroth all discuss how the patient's drivenness distances not only food but also all physical proximity and touch. The resulting isolation triggers hyperactivity and bulimia.[22] "Their greedy compulsive eating which often alternates with periods of ascetic abstinence, leads only to physical satiation, and leaves a psychic emptiness."[23] Somehow the space of freedom, specialness, and purification, found in her ego-less surrender to a psychic realm and invisible presence, turns to nothingness. As Binswanger describes it, "Ellen is alone, no longer flying in airy heights, but standing, with a frozen heart, on icy peaks."[24] It is as though there were a gate, one side of which is "cosmic surrender to the wind," the pneumatic psychic space, the other side of which is vast isolation and desolation. Hades entices her to the world of psychic depth which separates her from life attachments. From the underworld perspective, this is experienced as autarchy, detachment from the world of need, and magical ability.[25] From the upperworld perspective, this becomes death.

From above (and we see this not only in her symptoms but also in the research descriptions), the experience of the patient is inferiority, depression, extreme isolation, oppression. Bruch comments on this withdrawal and isolation: "The anorexics' appearance announces their loneliness. Giacometti's strange, emaciated sculptured figures are invariably interpreted as expressing remoteness and isolation."[26]

We have seen that the anorexic's "deficient ego" indicates the gift of interior space for vivifying and differentiating imaginal figures, for becoming nurse to, nourisher of, those figures. This capacity is what brings the tyrant to her in the first place. Yet with overidentification she becomes sucked dry by the tyrant figure; psychic experience turns to nothingness; she literally dies. But perhaps it is not the demonic figure per se but her relation to him vis-à-vis the upperworld which results in suffocation, void, literal death. From the dayworld perspective her experience of egolessness is felt as no-space, a nothingness which needs to be filled, completed. Nothing satisfies the void, so it becomes literal death. The emptiness is calling her to a place, a space. Psychologically, the emptiness is calling her to a metaphorical dying out of the personal which becomes an awakening to soul. Yet within the literalistic and materialistic perspective of the dayworld, this place remains "emptiness." Since she cannot see the tyrant as a metaphorical presence within soul, she literalizes him. Thus she starves herself and force-feeds others, and we see her as a literal, relentless nurse who has forgotten that she also can be psychological nurse to underworld presence.

This reminds us of our cultural neglect of the psychological nurse as caretaker and nurturer of image. This alternate view of nursing shows us how upperworld nurses may have lost their imagination. They have forgotten their relation to death and do not remember how to care for the psychic presences emerging from those suffering beside them. Nursing the dying also means being a companion to the inhuman presences which surround and beckon those leaving natural life. Perhaps the anorexic could remember her relation to the imaginal nurse through her memory of the child. Hillman reminds us that in the underworld the child, as the undivided force of life which "needs nursing and is nurse," is both sufferer and nurse.[27] The child represents an unfolding of new psychic life in that which is cut off, less than complete, immature. As child of Hecate, aware of her multiple perspectives, her intercourse with the imaginal realm, and her lack of personal differentiation, the anorexic might recall her ability as a borderline being to nurse underworld presences.

Perhaps we, too, to deepen our understanding of her affliction and literalization of psychic presence, should take a more
psychological look at it. How can we understand her refuges of
hyperactivity and bulimia? First we hear her tell us over and
over that she is not overactive, that her behaviors give her
energy and are not exhausting. According to our sense of time,
however, she is working overtime. Perhaps we should watch
her more closely. Maybe time for her is psychic movement
where there is no beginning or end or fast or slow in terms of
causality and linear progression. We ask why she is cleaning
the floor when she already cleaned it—as though what was
done before has a logico-temporal relation to what is being
done now. But that is our dayworld assumption about time.

From an underworld perspective we would not want to stop
or interrupt the repetitious activity but rather to enter it, since
it shows her working at an essential psychic level. So we ask: In
connection to what and whom is the tremendous amount of activity demanded? When we ask to what, with whom, does her
activity connect, we see that it takes her to the kitchen floor, to
the kitchen stove, to mother's purse, the grocery store, the
bakery. We see it sends her to buy food, to cook food, to serve
food, and compulsively to exercise it away. The tyrant drives
her through food to the realm of the mother.

Chapter IV
Mother of Skeletal Lady

Traditionally, the mother of the anorexic has seemed to be a bitch. Her symbiotic and destructive tie with the anorexic daughter has been determined as the starting point of the illness. One thing researchers consistently document: the anorexic's mother is domineering, demanding, frustrated, and ambitious. Let's examine specifically how the mother has appeared from the perspective of the researchers.

Meyer and Weinroth see an anxious and compulsive mother caught in a significant conflict with the daughter, resulting in the anorexic's oral fixation and general symptomatology. They interpret the negative rejecting qualities of the mother as the basis of the patient's attempt to reestablish the original mother–child unity (labeled "non-differentiation"), a desire "which is responsible for the multiple identifications which characterize these individuals." In their view, this goal of the patient to reestablish the mother–child fusion relates to her voracious consumption, which is opposed by a harsh superego.[1]

Nemiah observes "a peculiar relationship between the patient and her mother with a mixture of solicitous overconcern and aggressive domination. The mother and daughter form a restless and turbulent symbiotic unit."[2] Thoma holds this symbiotic bond responsible for the anorexic's autarchy and freedom from anxiety in the phase of the deathly starvation, since it can be seen as an "unconscious union with the imaginary picture of the beloved person. The patients live as though they were still unconsciously united to a nursing mother." This union with the mother's presence, he sees, leads to the patients' claims with "delusional insistence that they were 'their own providers,' and thus were not dependent on actual food supplies."[3]

So the "negative" qualities of the mother occur within a context of symbiotic non-differentiation which feeds the child more than concrete food. What is this "negative" of the mother which keeps the daughter in a place beyond personal and differentiated need? King describes the mother as "dominant" with an "irritable temperament." She is restrictive, and she tries to suppress the child's activity outside the family.[4] Theander considers the emotional immaturity and regression of the anorexic as resulting from ambivalent dependence on a difficult mother.

The mother of Anita (case 27) was "gloomy-minded" and dominating, often quarreled with her husband, and was always worrying about the children's health. Then Anita's "personality change" occurred: she became rigid and obstinate, would compulsively clean her room and do homework; she began to eat less, eat in secret (cucumbers in vinegar), and vomit when she had eaten too much. Her decreased eating resulted in problems with her mother. The relation to her mother was described as "ambivalent and full of conflicts." Hospitalized for severe headaches, Anita was observed to be anorexic, and she was diagnosed as depressed. She left the hospital after treatment with electroshock and antidepressive drugs and committed suicide.

Fanny (case 15) lived with her recently divorced mother in her maternal grandparents' home. The mother was extremely bitter and depressed after the divorce.

Fanny became more and more depressed and felt that she had only added to her mother's burden and that it would perhaps be better if she disappeared forever. She became religious and read the Bible and psalm book. This depressive reaction was accompanied by a loss of appetite. She felt as if she could not swallow the food and denied any feeling of hunger.

Elin (case 46) was an artist like her mother, to whom she was strongly attached. The mother was the dominating person in the family; the parents quarreled frequently. For several years, during which time she was anorexic, Elin kept company with a man of whom her mother disapproved. Elin committed suicide after three years of living with her mother a secluded life in which she slept during the day and was up at night. She could not "pull herself together to do any artistic work" during those years. Her mother became very depressed after Elin's death and was said also to have committed suicide.[5]

The child is contained, held in by a wounded but biting mother. The hypercritical and bitter mother is one who would over-protect the child, shelter her in symbiotic bliss, and this allows the daughter to merge with the mother's psyche. Blitzer et al. describe this initiation into the mother's dark psyche with an example: "Lisa's open depression, then, could be regarded as an expression of the mother's covert depression, which the mother could not directly express without a major breakdown in her defenses." They also note that the mother's death often precipitates the anorexia.[6]

The mother's "unintentional" initiation of the daughter into darkness is described in phenomenological detail in Bruch. The patients there speak of dreading the mother's empty and frustrated existence yet feeling a "special responsibility for their mother" and feeling inextricably bound to the mother's unfulfilled ambitions as well as to her criticisms.[7] The anorexic is the mother's confidante, and it is often the mother's physical disease or psychological breakdown which precipitates the "renewed clinging closeness" and subsequent anorexia during which the daughter feels compelled to stay with the mother.[8]

So it is this close mother whose "blackness" indeed propels the girl out of human life—to the night, to starvation, to the Bible, to black moods and compulsions. Out of body, home, and conventional daylight life: the mother beckons and embraces the child only to throw her out of this world.

We remember that "there is no other example of so close a relationship between mother and daughter" as that between Demeter and Persephone. Persephone, the maiden, was a kind of "duplication or continuation of Demeter."[9] At first Demeter also tried to keep her Persephone always at home with her, tied to the material earth, naively and innocently bound to the concrete beauty of the natural world. Yet this is when Persephone is introduced, through the maneuvers of Gaia, her great-grand-mother, to the world of death, the underworld. As much as Demeter, also called "the Angry One," would keep her innocent maiden out of darkness, Gaia arranges for the young one to know again the realm of destruction, once her own rightful domain.[10]

The Homeric hymn tells us that, while the Mother and Daughter temporarily are separated, Gaia, original Earth Mother of All Things, attracts and astonishes the Daughter, playfully picking flowers, with the beauty of a narcissus bloom. As Persephone reaches to grasp the flower, the ground begins to open—to gape—and she is seized by Hades who in a chariot carries her down to the underworld.

Earth's opening, her gaping mouth, brings us to another aspect of the patient's symptomatology. Recently, the medical and clinical understanding of the "dominant" mother motif has been related to aspects of feeding. Blitzer et al. add that the "disturbed" relationship between mother and daughter is reflected in oral fixations and feeding problems of the daughter.[11]

Dally and Gomez, as well as Kay et al., discuss the issue in terms of "mishandling" reflected in difficulties with infant feeding or in birth complications.[12] Bruch is the researcher who most thoroughly expands on this theme. She sees the mother's responses to the "child-initiated cues" as inappropriate; that is, the mother does not feed according to the child's needs but according to her own, so the child never learns to control her own bodily functions.

According to Bruch, this mother of the anorexic is a "gifted and frustrated" woman, a woman of potential achievement she sacrifices for the good of the family. Confined at home, she refuses to let the child wander away. Hence, the daughter who results from this protection never undergoes appropriate separation and is unable to perceive bodily signals or to individuate a personal differentiation. Unfulfilled ambition and inappropriate feeding contribute to the daughter's "non-differentiation."[13]

Like Bruch, Taipale et al., in "Anorexia Nervosa: An Illness of Two Generations," see the ambitions and intellectual needs of the mother as unfulfilled, see her caught in the home while trying to keep the daughter at home and rejecting any attempts of the daughter to rebel or become independent. Taipale maintains that the mother fears the daughter's adolescence and sexual maturity. The mother's fear becomes responsible for the child's anorexic symptoms and fixation at the oral stage:

> The child's wish not to become an adult is born in the mother; that is why the symptom oppresses the mother so much and brings out secondary conflicts. The mother cannot help her sick child when the latter is driven into the symptom but both of them find resonance on the level of oral symptoms and problems: in the illness of two generations.[14]

The child's wish not to become an adult is born in the mother. Mother wants daughter to remain literal child. Perhaps she is longing for the polymorphous nature of the child, the child's openness to the spontaneous multiplicity and engaging mystery of the imaginal world. Not able to look at these mysteries in her own darkness, mother holds on to child protectively. Mother wants eternal child yet would keep that child eternally on earth, confined to literal life, forever innocent. This appears in an upperworld perspective as "oral fixation" and "non-differentiation," yet it is precisely these aspects that we have seen compel the young girl to the underworld perspective—food takes her to psychic presence, and her egolessness is entry to the multiplicity of psyche.

From above, this situation looks like paradox, a "double binding" mother who is oversolicitous yet rejecting; who passes on her ambition, her desire to achieve, yet wants her daughter to stay at home, forever the natural child; who loves her genuinely yet hates her as separate from herself; who brings her to life yet forces her to death. From above we see a "black," obstinate mother who cherishes the ground the daughter walks on, who shows her the traps of the kitchen yet encourages her to eat, which makes her starve.

So mother's defense from psyche, denial of her own depths, sends daughter to psyche. As part of the syndrome, we have a bitter and breaking mother, strictly defended from her own wounds, who compulsively holds on to her daughter. This symbiotic bond allows daughter to enter, become privy to mother's void as well as to the bitter defense against it. Daughter gets caught between the depths of mother's darkness and the conscious attempts to defend against that abyss. We remember with Persephone and Demeter that the "clinging closeness" of the daughter and a mother who has denied or lost the underworld component accompanies entry to the void, the gaping mouth of earth's oral desire.

Hence, mother's symbiotic bond with daughter occurs with "inappropriate feeding," allowing daughter to enter into a realm outside the personal and natural and to consume the food of death. The mother does not feed the child with concrete food at appropriate dayworld times. With what does the mother feed the child? It is with *her* needs, her desires, her unfulfilled ambitions.

So it is not the home and the kitchen or the nonstimulating job in itself which is the "nonfulfillment" or the lack but rather mother's literal perspective and naturalistic hold on the world.

It is not cutting carrots, washing diapers, or dictating memos which keeps mother stuck and frustrated but the fact that she has lost the imagination, her underworld component, her metaphorical child who sees the world ensouled. Mother's form of mourning her loss is her defense of literally holding on to external child. The more mother tries to keep daughter at home, caught above with her in the naturalistic world, the more daughter consumes mother's nonfulfillments and absences and becomes the very thing mother lost: child of the underworld who resonates with imaginal presence, female who lives on nothing, skeletal mistress who reflects the realm of death to all living things.

The mother has lived too long aboveground, and she is co-opted by cultural pressures demanding she stay within the naturalistic perspective. She has lost her imagination and with it her 'fire,' her creative spark which nourishes as it stirs the intelligence of her heart's desires. She has lost underworld spark. Bored, she is not moved. Nothing stirs or delights a heart numbed; everything looks the same for years now, only senseless repetition of bleak day-in and day-out chores and assignments. Black stasis. She does not know what she wants because she does not know what she has lost. Unable to see through uniformity and conventionality, she has not seen that she has lost her desiring heart; the vitality of her heart's pulse is reduced to a dull ticking.[15] In a sense she wants her daughter to recognize the lack, whispering: don't grow, don't leave.

We ask: What is the telos, the inherent goal and fulfillment, of the mother's keeping the child home with her? What does mother wish daughter to see by keeping her that close? Does she want to prevent the girl from growing up forgetfully, in a way which would ignore or neglect her burning desires? Does she want her to know the mutual implication of mother/daughter, keeping both of them close to the wealth of the child's multiple identifications?

To blame or accuse the mother of the patient for this closeness or her defense, to see her as cause of the pathology, is to take our observations literally and deterministically, and then the external mother becomes a cause for the anorexic's symptoms. When we read the researchers' observations metaphorically, we see mother as one aspect of the constellation of this syndrome. The researchers think that mother's "gifts" are frustrated and directed onto food. Thus, mother's wealth is conveyed through food. What looks like "inappropriate feeding" becomes sustenance which binds daughter to mother's void, containing mother's hidden wealth, her "redirected gifts." Mother has been called to reclaim her place, now lost, in a realm outside naturalistic life yet has not been able to differentiate the wealth of this place and return it to life. Daughter is here to continue mother's "black" struggle.[16]

What the physicians and clinicians see as the fear of the mother and daughter of the daughter's adolescence and sexual maturity may also be mother/daughter's (unconscious yet literally enacted) understanding that maturity necessitates going backward too, returning to mother's ancient depths and placing them rightly. So mother's shadow, that part which is her lack, ignored, neglected, or denied for so long—her driving desires, her ambition, her underworld fury—emerges literally to seize and starve her literal child.

We have seen this figure. It is the tyrant. We spoke earlier of the tyrant as the dark, hidden side of the anorexic; now we see how this figure accompanies mother and mother's feeding. What looks from above like the unfulfilled ambition and inappropriate feeding of the mother seems from below to be the invisible presence who drives and feeds her. The mother has not been able to let this power in, so it emerges as dark shadow, as her "negative" side always there. With daughter as continuing sacrifice, the female is asked to recognize this shadow as sacred.

Chapter V
The Gaping Mouth

Anorexic Baby Food

When Demeter feels the loss of her daughter, seized by Hades and carried to the underworld, she takes on a "negative" stance. Grieving, she abandons food and drink, she does not bathe, and she searches the land for her daughter. After nine days, Hecate, appearing to her bearing light, tells Demeter she has heard Persephone being carried away but does not know by whom. Together they journey to the Sun who describes the abduction, observing that Zeus has permitted it. He tells Demeter her "vain and insatiate" anger does not suit her. Wounded, enraged with Zeus, Demeter withdraws from the company of gods. Rejecting the realms both of Olympus and Hades, she disguises her beauty and retreats into the human cities.[1]

We see here that the "negative" mother split from the underworld component—the psychic-mother aspect of every starving female—is enacting a form of Demetrean consciousness: by clutching the literalist upperworld side (retreat into human cities) and negating her loss (rejecting Olympus/Hades), she appears antagonistic, tyrannical, unfulfilled. This form of Demetrean consciousness bites as it mourns, hates the loss, tries to keep her child out of that underworld.

This Demetrean quality is the aspect of the anorexic which researchers have described as her "antagonism." The starving woman changes from a compliant girl to an antagonistic, "controlling bitch." But the opposite is always present: always surrounding Mother Demeter is her void, her loss. Beside the critical, restrictive, adult stance is that of the child enacting the realm of dream and death.

This void—the underworld which reverberates with imaginal presence, the mother's negative aspect, the part denied in the practical rule of the kitchen—starves the female as it seizes her. Through the very thing which ties her to personal mother in life—food—the starving female learns of the underworld, the realm of image. "Inappropriate" feeding keeps her bound to mother in such a way that she cannot avoid mother's shadow, mother's loss. She is nursed by the inappropriate in the mother, the shunned, the denied; she meets the tyrant.

So the nonfulfillment and antagonism of mother and the possession by tyrant accompany one another and co-exist for every starving woman. We have seen that a tyrannical side drives the starving female by way of food. One morsel carries demonic demands for her. The food of mother's mourning has brought her hellish images: food continually haunting, obsessing, compelling, bewitching her. Food becomes loaded with the accumulated fires of mother's unfulfilled desires.

So the daughter, tyrannically seized and starved, is carried to the world of invisible wealth and substance, forced to become open to the realm of image and essence beyond the personal and practical. But she fights this seizure, this possession, mourns it with a vengeful bite. The anorexic through her bond with the mother enacts Demeter's mourning as well as Persephone's abduction. The starving woman's bite, antagonism, and "insatiate angers" are fed by sources larger than her personal mother. The archetypal Mother is being called on here.

The upperworld view of the pathology recognizes that there is more involved with the mothering in this syndrome than the personal mother. One of Bruch's patients, described as being "too close to her mother and grandparents," attacked her mother with the accusation: "If I'm well, you won't love me anymore, you won't pay any attention to me." Bruch comments that actually the mother paid excessive attention to the daughter and suggests that more contact was needed with the father and the rest of the family.[2] Daughter wants mother's attention, but her personal mother gives it. So, to whom is she speaking? What archetypal Mother is being called?

Blitzer et al. see the mother of the anorexic to be strongly dependent on her own mother, a tie allowing the grandmother much authority over the child.[3] Selvini also states that the anorexic's maternal grandmother is demanding, hypercritical, possessive, and strong. The mothers of anorexics have served their mothers as "confidantes, servants, or nurses." Selvini cites Sperling who quotes Schwidder speaking of the harmful influence of the grandmothers, indicating that even when these grandmothers were not actually present in the family, or had been dead for years, "their dominating spirit and influence continued to prevail as alive as ever. The maternal grandmother's role may sometimes be assumed by the paternal grandmother." Selvini adds that the anorexic's mother also is fixated on a pregenital level of development and that the tie with her own mother prevents her from having a "real marital and maternal experience." Thus, she is a "highly ambivalent parthenogenic mother."[4]

Who is the powerful "dominating spirit" passing through these female generations? Is it not the figure who desires them to assume an underworld perspective which sees the essential and imaginal powers within all material life, who encourages them to live their desires vibrantly while imaginally? Is it not the figure who is stoking their creative fires, unused or abused? This figure of their unheeded, creative stirrings has turned "demonic" and appears again and again, asking for place, for recognition. This (Grand)Mother would allow the female to soar above or penetrate below the literal, naturalistic world, listening to essential themes, creating from them. The starving woman and her mothering know that her source of creativity is not dependent on phallic semen, yet she has not yet found her way down and through her seed which desires to blossom; she remains stuck in earth.

Unlike other forms of mothering, however, the mothering of the starving woman does not unconsciously live the loss: on one level mother is aware, and this awareness becomes her tyrannical bite. Her wound is in her understanding that she has lost her soul; her bite is in her understanding that she has not given up. If not worked through psychologically, this tension becomes literalized as *her* dominating nature, *her* hypercritical and controlling aspects.

This bite emerges as "negative mother": allowing her to force-feed or inappropriately feed the child who then inherits or becomes sacrifice to the invisible demon. This is the child who lives on nothing: no food, no emotion, no blood, no body. This becomes the starving daughter, sacrifice to the desires unfulfilled, our Mother's negative.

As long as the female denies the loss, refuses to let metaphorical death enter the kitchen, a starving part will embody tyrant, literally be seized out of life by tyrannical compulsions and rigidities. This tyrant side accompanies the aspect of the wailing and insatiate mother commanding her to come back to earth, to eat, be cured, become naturalistically normal.

The Chasm

After her rejection of Olympus and Hades and her retreat into the human cities, Demeter reaches Eleusis, ruled by Celeus. She looks withered and worn, appears as an old woman, a servant "beyond the gifts of Aphrodite." She comes to the Virgin's Well, where citizens of the town draw water. There she sits, taking in no food or drink. She looks up to see Celeus's daughters who have come to the well to draw water. They are inquiring about the old woman. She finds herself telling them that her name is Doso and that she was forced there from Crete against her will, with violence. The fantastic story unweaves: she was stolen by pirates, "arrogant masters" who would have sold her for a price, yet she managed to escape during their festivities and has wandered to Eleusis. She asks the young girls about work for an elderly woman, saying she could be a nurse or servant in someone's household.[5]

This story assists us in seeing how the starving woman is serving the chasm between female and imagination. The daughter aspect is ripped off and seized by the dictator Hades, lost to the underworld kingdom. We have seen that the anorexic carries death and image up to the living, finds her fertility and nurturance in the invisible, refuses to be bound literally to body, emotion, reproduction. But, ironically, the anorexic reflects the underworld perspective as she also mourns her loss of underworld components. We see this duality of aspects in the way her list of symptoms, as observed by the clinicians, is eerily close to Doso–Demeter. The anorexic literally starves (nine days without food and drink), she has little if any social/sexual intercourse as her skin and body dry up and wither (withdraws from the company of gods, disguises her beauty "beyond the gifts of Aphrodite," appears at the well as old woman). She lives undifferentiated, continually taken in by others' personalities/tastes/desires (captured by arrogant masters); she is irritable, feels no one understands her plight (was seized against her will); assumes an autonomous and even magical stance (boasts of barely escaping pirates); feeds or serves others, is generous (desires to be a nurse).

For a century, physicians and clinicians have treated these external manifestations of the Doso–Demetrean aspect. Yet the anorexic syndrome is an enactment of *both* the loss (where Persephone is) and the mourning (what Doso–Demeter does). The suffering of every starving woman is that the opening to the wealth of psyche *and* the tyrannical defense against that opening are her experience *at the same time*.[6] As much as food opens her to underworld potencies, she lives the defense against that realm, since she cannot see the metaphorical significance of food but focuses on its literal amounts, weights, and calorie contents.[7]

Perhaps now we can understand the transition when the anorexic's egoless entry into psychic space turns to suffocating void. As noted earlier, this 'space' relates to what researchers saw as her lack of ego differentiation: it is her ability to leave dayworld boundaries and cross to psychic realms. The experience is one of stepping into an abyss, and it is petrifying. In her egoless symbiosis with a personal mother, she has been able to turn away from the natural world and look to the depths, the gaping chasm, though she is scared to open her imagining eye to the psychic figures on the other side beckoning her to nurse them. Her connection with Mother allows the "non-differentiation" and entry to depths yet also bears the aspect of Doso–Demeter, warning her against those psychic realms.

With one foot at the chasm and peering down, she hears Doso–Demeter's cry and pulls back, obsessing or stuffing herself with matter in order to fill the void. But mother remains unfulfilled, and mother's loss itself emerges as fiery tyrant in literal food, returning her to the place where images feed. As the food begins to digest, its psychic significance fills her. Her vomiting and starvation reflect her commitment to explore the realm beneath and beyond the material.[8]

Thus, she returns to a skeletal existence, blindly enacting her ritual sacrifice. And this constellates Mother's grieving and angry voice: mother, monitoring a manic defense against death. Doso–Demeter calls her; again her space and speed become located in the kitchen, adhering to diet plans and weight programs, blindly and tyrannically gobbling, cleaning for, stealing from Mother.

So daughter, like mother, knows the numbness of the void where repetitions (starving/gorging/vomiting) become another monotonous task of Hell. She cannot yet see the psychic value to which food beckons, is blind to the ritual of this enactment.

Food objectified and literalized becomes tasteless as it takes larger and larger quantities of it or absences from it to let her sense anything at all. The insatiability of Doso–Demeter is that possession does not satisfy yet tyrannically consumes her.

The starving woman's desire to be nourished by realms outside the immediate and concrete accompanies an identification with a tyrannical, material aspect which calls her home, wishes her to see food only as inanimate matter. As sacrifice to the Mother's negative side, she is being asked to make sacred the female's potent underworld attributes yet has been caught in life's fixities like Doso–Demetrean Mother, crying and beckoning (herself) to return from death, to keep from soul.[9]

Physicians and Clinicians: Attend

This aspect of Doso–Demeter, caught in the chasm separating the woman from the vitality and resonance of an imaginal world, has been appearing in another form all through our study, not simply in the 'darknesses' of personal mother and the literalization of food and antagonisms of starving daughter. One hundred years of research also reflect this tyrannical consciousness. We have seen that upperworld researchers have called starving females back to life by denying their entry into metaphorical death. The doctors are in the grip of wailing Demeter: she would pull back the young daughter by viewing her as the frail, innocent one, trying to keep her the nubile, earthly flower-child. They, too, have kept their distance from her even as they force-fed her, tugging her up to their naturalistic perspective.

In this medical attitude, we see the counterpart of Hades' rape of Persephone. That anorexics are tied and shocked, given antidepressants, put on reinforcement contingency schedules, forced to undergo leucotomies and tubefeeding (resulting for many in suicide or a worsened condition) shows them less victims of psyche than of a one-sided, naturalistic perspective.

Cure is defined as a return to the conventional female: increase in weight, development of secondary sexual characteristics, improved attitude toward eating, return of menstruation, social adaptation. Thus, the anorexic is seen as incurable: the more they try to put earth back in her, the more she dies.[10] No place is given to the metaphorical significance of mother's loss, and so it becomes tyrannical, demonic, its desire literalized in actual death.

We have allowed a place for the medical perspective, but it has not let in ours. Physicians and clinicians have not followed the starving woman to the regions of her "regressions" and her "drive disturbances." Doctors have not let the personified voices speak through her, so these—the psychic figures who are her gift and grace—must suffocate her, starve her, send her back and forth from Hades to the kitchen, until we listen, look, and attend. Attend: not monitor her hypothalamus, not stimulate her gastrointestinal tract, not regulate her diet but attend to them, the ones for whom she truly is medium and carrier, to the psychic figures—mother, tyrant, and compliant maiden of innocence.

In the clinical and medical approaches, we find a continual attempt to return the starving woman to 'reality,' convention, to a 'normal' female body. No attempt is made to enter her pathology, find the root metaphor within it. Where there is rigid repetition and defensive literalization, the physicians and clinicians might look for the rape, for there is a psychic rape, a possession by a psychic figure, occurring. No attempt is made to look through the defense to explore the possessing figures. Instead, standing on naturalist terra firma, the researchers pronounce the starving woman a child of magical thinking, inferior, stunted, and regressed. Examples of this medical approach are everywhere; we shall focus on two.

From the upperworld perspective, the imaginal reality of the anorexic is not reality at all but fantasy, and thus it must be corrected. It is called "denial." One group of psychiatrists (Gottheil et al.) attempted to cure anorexia by readjusting the patient's body image (her sense that her skeletal form was regular and pleasing). They considered this body image as wrong, as a denial of literal "reality," and attempted to alter her self-image by developing "a more objective view of herself." This occurred "against a great deal of resistance" and even hostility and self-destruction on the part of the patient.[11]

Their procedure was based on SIE (self-image experience) sessions in which the patient was shown a motion picture film of herself responding in an interview. This was followed by a set of questions about her reactions to the film. Eventually, after suicide attempts, chemotherapy, and constant supervision, the patient came to respond "realistically" to the film. That is, she noted the difference between the mirror view, in which she did not see herself as emaciated or ugly and was pleased with her skeletal appearance, and the film, in which she saw the thinness "objectively" and said she looked "sickly." The authors report that they corrected her "denial" (that she looked normal or even fat and not emaciated) which previously was so strong it withstood pleas from the family, evidence from the mirror, and two hospitalizations. As a result the "distorted self-image" shifted "in the direction of increased reality."[12]

What happened here to the aspect of the female who genuinely saw herself as fat, the world of the fat-starving woman? The researchers note that at one point the patient began to pull out some of her hair saying: " 'There is something inside of me that I have to get out and I don't know what it is. I feel angry at myself.' " She became confused and behaved in response to the "voice of her own mind. The voice told her she did not have the right to look at magazines and daydream of being like the healthy, well-dressed pretty young women she saw in advertisements."[13]

No one helped her to hear the rapacious voice with its demands, to contain and give form to its metaphorical expression. Instead, she had to cut her forehead and pull out her hair so she would not be pretty; she enacted the demands of the voice, became identified with the voice, was raped by it. All this was "corrected" with constant supervision and SIE retraining; yet the "voice," unattended, was left lingering until its next possessive interchange with the woman.

A second example pertains to the work of Hilde Bruch.[14] She sees the anorexic as fixed at an early stage of development; she wants to make the patient mature. Maturation is related to ego-differentiation. Bruch recognizes that the anorexic is in a place which makes her feel "special," that the starving accompanies "inner psychic experiences"; yet from an upperworld stance she defines this place in terms of ego defects, lack of differentiation, "interpersonal disturbances and developmental deficiencies," and "self-deceptions."[15] Yet these aspects keep the anorexic close to soul, and to "cure" them is perhaps a defense against soul.

Bruch sees the dangers of external manipulative approaches to pathology. She criticizes behavior modification programs, stating that the "underlying problems" have to be explored.[16] In some of her descriptive work, she begins to enter the anorexic's psychic territory and shed light on the sights, smells, voices, and movement of that realm (for example, in chapter 5 of *The Golden Cage*). But then, in a medical-clinical perspective, she directs us how to remove the patient from those realms. Her program of ego-differentiation and maturation tries to bring the anorexic out from the depths while denying them, to bring the patient back to earth through "Changing the Mind" (chapter 8, *The Golden Cage*).

She recognizes that the anorexic is carrying the parental, particularly the maternal, struggle. Yet instead of seeing the inherent necessity in this, or the means to move the anorexic in and through it, she urges the parents to keep their problems to themselves.[17] This is valuable in the sense that it removes the focus from external variables as causal to the illness, yet there is no further exploration of the anorexic psyche itself. The focus of this program is more on correction and repair than on deepening the anorexic's psychological world:

The task of psychotherapy in anorexia is to help a patient in her search for autonomy and self-directed identity by evoking an awareness of impulses, feelings and needs that originate within her. Therapeutic focus must be on the patient's failure in self-expression, on the defective tools and concepts for organizing and expressing needs, and on the bewilderment in dealing with others. Therapy represents an attempt to repair the conceptual defects and distortions, the deep-seated sense of dissatisfaction and isolation, and the conviction of incompetence.[18]

"Your expression 'I hate myself if I gain weight' is a dramatic example of such an erroneous assumption. There is nothing hateful about you or your body. When I say something like that you seem to agree but you don't truly believe it. In this way we miss the real problem, and you don't explore the background of this false conviction. As long as you are absolutely determined not to argue, you'll cling to your secret convictions. As far as learning or changing anything goes, it's a dead end."[19]

The assumption here is that the anorexic world is based on defects and distortions which have to be eradicated. The focus on "self-direction" precludes exploration of the images, voices, and dreams within the "isolation, and conviction of incompetence." The imagistic reality within which she stands and lives is ignored and, worse, denigrated; the gulf between grieving and bitter mother and her underworld child still looms very large.

Repairing the anorexic by turning her into a mature, self-focused adult, no longer beckoned by realms outside the naturalistic, trains her out of her mysteries, cuts off what tenuous connection she holds (for the Mother's sake) with the underworld child. Nevertheless, given Bruch's devotion to the anorexic, the years she studied this figure when there were few cases to be found, as well as her decades-long, detailed study and descriptions, we can imagine her as relating to the patient at the level of the metaphorical child starving and screaming for attention.

In one small passage, she speaks of meeting the patients (who, she states, generally lack humor) on a lighter level, in a "friendly, well-meaning way," to assist in the exploration of their cynical and negativistic world.[20] Though she is trying to erase the tyrannical demon, train the stunted child to grow up and out of erroneous assumptions and false convictions, in a sense she can be said to be touching and even nursing the child-within-the-tyrant.

In any case, the mysteries of the realm beckoning the anorexic patient have not been studied and delineated carefully in themselves. Instead of finding which archetypal personae reside in syndrome and diagnosis, *both* patient and doctor literalize the complexes. Bruch remarks how easily the therapist becomes constellated as the domineering, force-feeding mother.[21] Now that the profession is alert to that, the literalization has moved to the actual parents. Putting mother and father in a room and discussing blocks in communication keep it all aboveground.[22] This family therapy is probably safe for the therapist but more literally deadly for the anorexic than the psychic world of death with which she is so familiar.

Chapter VI
Gaia's Sickle

We are grateful, in a sense, for the symptoms of the starving woman and for the way they have refused to be stifled or cured for a century. They will not let go of her, and through her the culture, until they take us deeper into psyche. There is something here demanding recognition.

After all, here we have one who has denied all principles of matter—food, body, blood—and the fixities of dayworld consciousness—space, time, linearity—and shifted to the reality of the psyche.[1] She enacts in her disease the interpenetration of the imaginal and physical realms. By starving, she also starves the culture of its conventional fantasy of the female. No longer a receptive, silly, and timid girl full of hope and wonder, she carries us away from the natural perspective of food and blood and body to the underworld where she becomes active, potent, autonomous, capable of endless work.

We also have seen that her entry into psychic territory has not been fluid or conscious; instead, she has been ripped out of life, tyrannized by an inner force which rigidly possesses her. And in her desperate attempt to keep one foot on earth, she literalizes the tyranny—deals with it exclusively with materialistic solutions, real food.

Now we want to know more about the mytheme within her syndrome. Whose world is she unfolding? To what, to whom can her syndrome be likened? What is the root metaphor of her pathology? We must follow her backwards and downwards: to recover the place and the Gods to whom her affliction refers. Without reductionist and nominalist matching or classification, we ask and we wait. We have been seeing and hearing it all along.

We have seen a starving woman fed by the invisible shadows of the underworld, seen her, a skeleton from the dead, nursing others. Through her 'neurotic' repetitions and hyperactivity, we witness the pull between dayworld consciousness and underworld perspective. We recall that, as much as the Doso-Demetrean mother wants to keep it all aboveground, the original Mother Gaia opens for the offspring to descend. The original parthenogenetic Mother Gaia: has she not been here all along, and does she not return us to our starting point? Gaia herself has come, choosing the starved wraith to enact her desire and recover the Mother's rightful place in the underworld.

Patricia Berry reminds us that Great Mother Gaia is the original progenitor of all the other divinities, including Zeus, Poseidon, and even Hades. As such, Gaia is as comfortable with the perspective of the underworld as with the natural life of the upperworld. For her the two realms are not in opposition. Berry examines how Gaia's split from her underworld aspect occurs by the upperworld becoming the place of Ge–Demeter, the underworld being served by Ge–chthonia, the place of Persephone. As the chasm between maiden and earth mother widens, it is Gaia who opens up to provide young Persephone to descend into a new vision of things, imaged by Hades' rape.[2] Mother knows best. From our upperworld perspective, it would be too easy to conceptualize this in terms of a necessary literal rape, of male seizing and initiating female and literally dragging her down. Yet if we stay close to the mythic figures, we see Gaia's desire and her opening as the ground of it all.

Gaia starves us as women and obsesses us with starving in order to send us to the depths. Gaia remembers what appears as the negative of the Doso–Demetrean mother, the aspect of mother which knows she has lost her underworld fertility yet does not know how to regain it. So Gaia faces her with repetitious starving, compelling her away from a naive relation to matter. Yet the female has not yielded to the imaginal realm surrounding the tyrannies of food and body. Instead we find starving woman seemingly rigid and unresponsive. And, for over a century, doctors also resisting Gaia's message have been trying to revive starving woman, warm her, keep her aboveground, fill out her curves, circulate her blood and milk once again.

Yet Gaia has not let her be cured. Keeping oneself above it all by being substantially fed by the grain of the earth is not Mother's desire. Gaia knows that Mother has been identified too long with wailing Demeter and the literalization of earthly things. This is not Mother's desire; it is even sinful, precisely because Ge–Demeter herself is sick to her stomach with the gross physicality of her own nature.

Gaia is trying to recover the chthonic spirit Hillman sees in Hades (opposed to the materialism of mother) yet which is present also within her. She knows she is simultaneously material, maternal earth *and* the chthonic void with its own spirit, necessity, and essential patterning. She elects the starving woman to enact her desire. Mother has been cut off from the underworld for too long and she is starving—she needs to be fed by the shades, craves the invisible food of the imagination. She is fed up with upperworld naiveties and fixities and starves for the underworld and imaginative fertility.

This literalization and longing are expressed in great numbers of women by the dogged domesticity which often accompanies starving obsessions. Weighed down with bodily and material things, they are so burdened by the emptiness of the starving of their souls that they can barely get out of bed. Culture says: she's depressed, she's agoraphobic. The accumulating void 'blackens' and paralyzes her: like Doso–Demeter, she knows she has lost something but does not know how to regain it; knows she is starving but does not know how to get fed; sees the calorie counts everywhere, has lost sight of what things look like, taste like; she snaps at the children uncontrollably when they get chocolate on the rug.

Eventually, only an acting-out of ferocious rage or soaring ambition (she now runs the office with topnotch efficiency) can tear the woman out of her suffocating void. Now her starvation speaks in a language of frenzied activity. Culture says: she's hysterical, she's a bitch. In either case, suffocating in fixed earth or burning in hell's fires, she is starving, not fed by the waters of the soul, empty, not touched or stimulated by the movement of the imagination. Gaia, in allowing us so blatantly to suffer our starvation, seems to be announcing that it is time to use our sensitivities to lower ourselves into the underworld's "hidden waves,"[3] be soothed and nourished as we carry it all up again in creative endeavor.

So Mother wants down. She wants to reenter the underworld which was once her rightful domain. She wants us to remember Hades as her offspring. So within the economy of Gaia, metaphorical feeding becomes sacred. The identification of the female with food, emotion, and reproduction becomes sinful, and eating must be followed by complicated purification ceremonies to eject the harmful materials. For Gaia, exclusive identification with literal matter is the crime.

The tyrannies of the starving woman serve as the imaginal location of the Demeter–Persephone mytheme in our culture. It is the pathology serving the quest of the earthbound mother, her lost underworld daughter, as well as the grief and anger accompanying their schism. We have seen the anorexic as deathly lady aboveground, showing us the death within life (the Persephone within Demeter), and also as nurse to the underworld figures, reflecting the multiplicity of the soul and invisible fertility (the Demeter within Persephone). Yet we have seen her driven by the tyrannical Hades force, responding to the call of the Doso–Demetrean mother in the kitchen to gorge or obsess over food details. If she is enacting Persephone's journey here, one thing clearly emerges: it is not an easy transition for her from below to above and back. She has forgotten Persephone's sacred rituals allowing a fluid psychological transformation. For we have seen that this fair one is tossed to and fro between a compulsive tyrant and a grief-stricken and resistant mother. Beginning as a sacrifice to allow the mother to become connected to her "unfulfilled ambition," her invisible drive and original psychic potency, the starving woman has become trapped in the vicious opposition of upper- and under-worlds.

In this she reflects the problem of the culture: Mother is split from Hades, and Father still dominates the realm beyond life. The starving woman has become victim of this chasm—here to cross it for us yet die because of it. In refusing to keep the realm of Mother tidily compact on earth in sugary niceties of "femininity," she has broken herself down to the doorway of a perspective informed by soul and death, yet she is caught at the threshold. Instead of conjoining the realms of Mother and Father, she has lived the material concretisms in literally suicidal and tormented ways.

The death and disease of starving women testify that the chasm between the 'female' of materialist upperworld identity and the 'male' of psychic underworld realities is so broad that Mother and Father may never speak to one another. The gap also implies that commerce between the two will be experienced as an abysmal drop, a violation.[4]

This is reflected by the psychoanalytic interpretations of anorexia which state that the anorexic's fear of eating is due to her equating eating with oral impregnation. One of these interpretations,[5] drawing from the dreams and fantasies of an anorexic patient, discusses anorexia (and what currently is called bulimia) as the desire to castrate the father and give the phallus to the mother to secure her support and protection. Eating is a symbolic act of oral castration; vomiting and starvation are the disgust at her desire. Some analysts state that this desire to emasculate and displace the father to please the mother is an attempt by the anorexic to strengthen the primary oral-dependent bond with the mother. She returns to this primal union with the mother by passing the phallus from father to mother. Through this she serves to revive the mother's procreative properties and potencies.

Consequently, the anorexic daughter uses the phallus to bring mother to a primal, essential place prior to and permeating dayworld reality. This return relates to the descriptions, in the literature, of both mother and daughter as having a parthenogenetic nature.[6] Primal union with mother refers to the place before birth, prior to life, the place of the essential dead, where the woman becomes connected to patterns and "waves" underlying the physical and immediate, connected to an underworld potency.

Yet the Freudian imagination here conceives of the relation to this realm of the "*dead* life"[7] by the anorexic and the mother in terms of the transmission of the phallus. It sees female autarchy and potency only in terms of a transference of the father's phallus. This view reminds us that entry to the realm of death for over two thousand years has been through and conveyed by the phallus.

The psychoanalysts are stuck in the same oppositional thinking which traps and binds the starving woman herself. It is not within the purview of their clinical research that the woman's body itself, her food and her fertility, can connect her to underworld potencies. Her materialistic aspects are viewed as inherently opposed to underworld mysteries embodied in the phallus, so any connection between the two (female and the underworld) necessitates seizure and possession of the phallus. Ignored here is the hidden seed of the pomegranate, and forgotten is the climax of the Eleusinian Mysteries: when Persephone announced her rule over the dead, there was displayed an ear of wheat.[8]

This chasm between female and underworld continues to devour and possess women today. The starve–gorge cycle shows the woman trying to blend or merge black mother with red father—yet this is not a creative conjunction. That blackness is acted out with a heat that suggests the scorching following flames: compulsions go wild, and what is left is charred. Her body is burned in the consumptive fire, left a black skeleton.

Starving woman has not seen how the realms interpenetrate, imply one another while remaining distinct. All along we have seen that in every starving woman is one who potentially can be a lady of borders, who can experience the double nature of upperworld and underworld. Yet overidentifying with the psychic figures precludes participating in their interpenetration. Her message that death exists always as metaphor within life is lived as literal starvation. Her message that Mother can become nurse to underworld configurations gets literalized into forcing her family to eat dinner. The starving woman bears the message of Gaia but keeps it literally enacted. It is the oppositional and literal stance of the starving woman (and of the culture) which necessitates seizure by the psychic figures. At least she has drawn close to them, yet simultaneously she has adopted the culture's resistance and materialistic bias, keeping the chasm alive. She needs to step down into the psychic regions, and educating her in such a descent would allow this to happen through the body and not at its expense.

How might one guide the starving woman to understand the message and implications of her compulsions? The psychoanalytical fantasies carry us to a primordial castration. But where they interpret, we shall not; rather, we shall keep an ear to the sound of the myth, hear how it resonates. There we hear a primordial castration also, but one which does not involve the transmission of Father's seed but instead carries us to the seed of the female.

We have heard that even Gaia at one time became burdened by her own materialism and maternalism. Gaia's firstborn was Ouranos, the starry sky, and through her nightly intercourse with him she brought forth many children. Yet, when it came time to give birth to the three most terrible sons, who from the beginning hated their father, Ouranos would push them back inside Gaia.

Gaia, who "groaned within for pressure / or pain," created "the element of gray flint / she made of it a great sickle." Her son, "devious-devising Kronos," agreed to help her in her release "and giant Gaia / rejoiced greatly in her heart / and took and hid him in a secret ambush / and put into his hands / the sickle, edged like teeth, and told him / all her treachery and huge Ouranos came on / bringing night with him, and desiring / love he embraced Gaia and lay over her / stretched out / complete, and from his hiding place his son / reached with his left hand / and seized him, and holding in his right / the enormous sickle / with its long blade edged like teeth, / he swung it sharply, / and lopped the members of his own father, / and threw them behind him / to fall where they would."[9]

When Gaia was stuffed to the brink with her offspring, she made a sickle out of flint and used it to remove the weight of her accumulating materialism. Mother's intelligence and her creative use of the flint sickle allowed the mass of weight to differentiate itself into Gods and Titans, who were then placed above and under the earth.[10]

So Mother has the means to move out from under the weight of materialism. She has her own weapon and source of destruction. The utensil for harvest, the tool for collecting crops, has another edge. The starving woman knew all along the mystery of the kitchen knife—that it can be used to cook as well as butcher. The mother serving stuffed Gaia knows that the implement keeping her fixed to the kitchen offers her a way out.

This movement requires going through the fixedness and blackness of Kronos,[11] not around it. Kronos relates to the 'darkness' each starving woman has inherited from her literal mother in the first place. Kronos is the one who "devours his own children, is the divinity who, through time and death, causes 'that which becomes' to return to its formless origin."[12] For the starving woman and, the literature tells us, for her mother too, Kronos has entered and has had a hand in it all.

Mother perhaps has lived Kronos literally by her bite, her dark moods and depressions. We have to be grateful for our mother's darknesses since they at least have moved us out of the innocent whitenesses of Pollyanna flirtatiousness.

But the starving woman has not been educated consciously and delicately to go through this Hell in order to delineate the boundaries and colors of soul. Instead, hellish torments have been acted out as an external drama of the stomach. Today's starving women, loyal to their mother's unanswered questions,[13] have moved a generation closer to the potencies of this underworld but for the most part have been fixated in Kronos blackness, have not been able to use grandmother's sickle to slice through the dark and sort out the Gods.

Instead of being acted out literally, the blackness has to be worked with psychologically. We use the sickle which places the Gods in their proper psychic territory by dialoguing with and going through the Kronos darkness. Unless it is worked psychologically, woven into our psychic tapestry, the blackness tips too easily to red, and this oscillation of rigid black fixities and red compulsions consumes the woman.[14]

Sickles divide and separate; a sickle is a cold, hard metallic instrument which cuts to the quick. As therapists and friends, we must allow the starving woman her hard sickle, the crescent made of metal which sparks as it bites, allow her the cold and antagonistic places of suspicions, hurts, hatreds all exposed. We must let the cold, metallic sickle be her instrument, or she will remain virginal in the sense of naive and innocent. An imaginal therapy would give her separation, a slicing from her own compulsive desires and repetitious tyrannies, so that she could contain, reflect, and place them, instead of *being* them. Sickle through them: her possession by the tyrannical shapes of soul weighs her down, forces her into the rigid repetitions. Through an imaginal therapy, these possessing figures would be sliced apart from body and food.

Chapter VII
Imaginal Therapy

Female Seed

What is the sickle? Is it Mother's way out of the pressures and pains of her binding materialism, her way down to psychic depths connecting her with the seed of the underworld? What is the means by which the Mother of All Things regains her throne in the underworld? The image of Mother with sickle returns us to the "negative mother," and through it we see that the tyrant is *within* the mother herself. It is only when upper and underworlds are split that griefstricken earth mother and pernicious tyrant are constellated as opposites. The sickle means that the underworld does not have to oppose or be opposed, that the underworld no longer has to emerge through possession by a demonic Hades.

So we wonder how, through the creative force of her weapon, Mother relates daimonically[1] to the underworld. Gaia's sickle releases, differentiates, and materializes the gods. It is the instrument for realizing the psychic powers within the material world. Conscious engagement with these figures can be revitalizing and nourishing, can cut through the "demonic" possession which up to now has been the only way the woman could 'know' them.

But starving woman is afraid of consciously yielding to the psychic powers. Even when they clamor so loudly in her symptoms, she resists the message. Along with Doso-Demeter, she clings to the naturalistic perspective to avoid what looks like death in the awakening of her own soul. What is demanded when the violated skeleton emerges metaphorically in the therapy room is a psychological transformation, a conscious awakening to the underworld powers residing within life. Carefully residing within the myth of Demeter-Persephone[2] can assist here.

We saw that the dark Demetrean rigidity and resistance accompany fiery possession by a tyrannical force. Though it moves the starving woman in opposite directions (starve-gorge), the literalism in both thrusts is similar. The opposites always touch. For the woman to gain ensouled body, both have to yield. Demeter's material fixity has to know itself also as image; Hades' volatilities and desires have to embody themselves, find 'legitimate' ground. This yielding is less a merging or balancing than an assimilation each of the other, an absorption of the other without either losing itself.

The myth describes in detail this yielding of Demeter/Hades. We left Demeter at the Well of the Virgin in Eleusis, sitting in her age, beginning to draw in her senses. This is the beginning of Demeter's "death," her "dying to the world." Her consciousness turns inward, yet such a first "turning away from the outward world is experienced as a *nox profunda*."[3] She begins to draw from inward powers, collecting herself in her age, metaphorically drawing from her virginity, the impersonal ancient wellspring. As an elderly nurse, she enters Metanira's home with the four daughters. This is a first move inward, a mode of separation, containment.

This well goes deep but is cold and dark. Demeter is beginning to draw from the well of the psychic abyss. Here we have the 'pause' necessary for any move out of gripping compulsions or obsessions. Starving woman is alone, withered, empty; she reaches out to grab food delights yet, if she pauses, within the silence she may hear waters stirring in ignored depths. Let her sit in the embrace of her own female nature, damp and unfamiliar, sit with it. Some young thing with a plan will emerge. The waters are moving.

The therapeutic move into a contained vessel to explore the nightmare is one manifestation of drawing from the well of the virgin. When men have become pirates, when tyrants abound, it is time for virginal withdrawal. Preferably the vessel will be housed with other women, nurturing and giving. This is the first move of the woman out of public, external spheres to stay with her own inherent coldness, her griefstricken nature, hearing its cries resound from the spring waters of earth's hollow depths. In the void of her own stillness, the psychic analogies to her previously lived hyperactivities will begin to well up.

Therapeutically, this withdrawal corresponds to entering the inherent cold of the starving woman, allowing her a separation from some of life's attachments, allowing her a room of her own. We see Demeter enacting this separation upon entering Metanira's home. Sitting on the silver fleece, hardened in her grief, refusing food and drink, she waits, veiled. This waiting allows silver-reflection of her cold back to herself. She is "wasting away with longing / for her daughter / in her low dress."[4] At precisely this point most starving women act out literally, resorting to compulsions and hyperactivities to avoid the implied void. It is very difficult to sit with one's frozenness behind a black veil, since eventually it is longing which unfolds and the longing goes so deep. Demeter does sit with the longing; virginal movement ripples from beneath. The daughter Iambe/Baubo[5] charms and humors her with obscene stories and gestures.[6]

Interesting here is the suggestion that, from other women and the female guides of our soul, we can yield to the mysteries of the underworld in ways less consuming, direct, violating. Woman to woman, we can ease ourselves to the presence of psychic figures running between, moving through us. We can know of the underworld in a style untouched, virginal, yet which runs deeper, is truer to the death of that realm than the acting-out afforded by most heterosexual education. We need to find our ancestral virgins, the wise, sacred females of our imaginal landscape. They move us to soul, they make us smile.

Demeter submits to and laughs at Iambe/Baubo's provocative humor. Black rigidities begin bending to heart and humor. Her jaw loosens, eyes light up. She knows to refuse the sweet red wine offered by Metanira, instead asking for some water with barley and pennyroyal.[7]

When the starving woman smiles, she can begin to play with her female companions and begin to know and discriminate her appetite. She sees that a direct assimilation of wine, the drink of Dionysus/Hades, is not for her. She knows it is too sudden an assimilation of that underworld force. To take it in such an abrupt and consumptive manner is analogous to the seizure by Hades, the underside of his rape. So there has to be an *education* in soul, rather than immediate descents. With humor she begins to extricate herself from the blind seizures and compulsions. Wine is not her drink but rather barley, grain of the earth, with a touch of mint. She chooses a softer, more delicate nourishment. She can move to death *through* keeping to her own taste.

Metanira recognizes that there is uncommon blood in Demeter and offers her the child, her son Demophoön, to care for, entrusting everything she has to Demeter. With her sweet breath and anointings of ambrosia, Demeter begins to nurse the child. At night she holds the child in a powerful fire to make him immortal like a god. One night the spying Metanira sees this. She wails: "Baby Demophoön, / the stranger / hides you in all that fire / and makes me weep / and brings me bitter pain." Demeter's response is fury. She announces to Metanira that the latter's stupidity and blindness have prevented her son's gaining immortality.[8]

We see from this episode that the Demetrean aspect which is moving out of a rigid upperworld stance has to kindle the child, lower it to flame. Within the void of her own soul, Demeter has found the spark of humor which has ignited the child. She must teach the fretful mother that the child has to know the fire of what to us looks like death in order to be worthy. She has to teach another what she earlier could not see: that the child must not remain innocent in life, must enter the mysteries of death or soul, the place beyond life. She is showing Metanira that the child is not her own personally, cannot be if she is to become an intimate of the fire of the Gods.

Through this spark of a fire spirit, Doso–Demeter is entering psychic reality, is seeing the child through a "critically imagining eye";[9] she is letting go of her literalist stance, handing it over to the Gods. This is part of what must be done in the education of starving woman: burn the child, ignite the child. Baubo's humor is not playful like soap bubbles and hopscotch; it is obscene. Set fire to the innocent delight in earthly simplicities; spark the imagination within each of her material solutions.

Knowing the child as child-of-fire ignites the starving woman's "borderline" existence and her denial of dayworld classification, her potential openness to a world animated, to the multiple figures in a world shimmering in imaginal configurations (Elsa's "frightening mental images," Ellen's imaginal presences, the "phantom phenomena" of Bruch's patients). Perhaps, to purify essence from the child, we have to go to the old places where the child has been burned, the ancient wounds, letting the childhood diseases, hurts, and inferiorities open starving woman to the Gods in her fate.

Once Demeter teaches another mother the necessary connection to immortal fire, she is ready for her altar, her mysteries, and a new form of rage has the effect of reconnecting her with her daughter, her underworld component. Her rage and beauty now have potency outside of human limits and scope. She announces that she is the goddess Demeter. She names herself. Then she requests that a huge temple be built for her, stating that there she will inaugurate the mysteries. As she says this, her size and shape change; beauty and fragrance take the place of literal old age.

In her temple, Demeter stays far away from the other gods, still longing for her daughter, and now her longing breeds action. She conceals the seed in the earth. Zeus summons her first through the goddess Iris, then through the other gods, sending beautiful gifts to persuade her back to Olympus, thus to prevent the famine which might destroy all humans. Demeter refuses: "no one/was able to persuade / her mind and heart/ because she was furious/inside,/and she rejected/their words/ cold./For she said/she would not ever again/set foot/on fragrant Olympus,/she would not/let the fruit of the earth/come up/until/she saw with her eyes/her daughter's/beautiful face." Zeus then sends Hermes to arrange a reconciliation, to bring Persephone back from the underworld to her mother.[10]

Demeter's temple corresponds to a further retreat from the adhesion to the physical world; now she is guided by the mysteries of her sacred nature. Dying to the world led her to sit with her longing, which has opened the fires of her soul. For Demeter to reconnect with the daughter she must place herself in a temple, see the sacredness of her attempt to find the essence of her woundedness. Now the longing becomes a form of prayer.

Female has seed, too. The way for a female to remember the connection with the underworld is to stay close to her seed; Demeter does this through a penetrating form of female rage. "Concealing the seed" is a form of rage which does not pertain to eradicating the immediate enemy, initiating warfare, or setting up a paranoid defense system. It relates instead to sitting still and locating the power, Mother's creative force, inward. It pertains to remaining contained in and opening up to the beauty of the interior world, the depth of the imagination, the seed of that.

Whereas Demeter was reactive and barren at the well, her isolation and yielding to humor and fire-spirit have given her an autonomous potency and fertility. She contains herself as she conceals her seed. Still behind the black veil, now she is in sacred terrain; the seed is germinating. She is active; she knows what she wants; she holds her ground. Her blackness is no longer rigid and inert; it has loosened, yielded, *yet it has not lost its firmness.* In surrendering to soul, she is activated in isolation, and this inner movement has an outer effect.

Further, the Demetrean aspect knows not to settle at this time for the false flatteries or cajoling promises of advancement or gift but rather to wait until the daughter is returned. Even the messenger Iris, the in-between lady who complies with Zeus's commands, a transporter of others' affairs, does not convince her. Demeter has been through too much to fall for Iris; she is not going to comply or mediate a harmony. Her seed remains concealed.

When Hermes reports to Hades that Demeter is isolated, sitting in terrible anger, concealing the seed in the ground, and that Persephone must be returned, Hades obeys the commands of Zeus, telling Persephone: "'Go on, / Persephone, / back to your mother / in black veil, / go with a kind heart. / Do not despair / too much: / it is useless. / As a husband / I will not be/ unworthy of you / among the gods: / I am the brother of your father. / Zeus. / When you're here, / you will reign / over everyone who lives / and moves, / and you will have / the greatest honors / among the gods. / And there will be / eternal punishment / for those who do wrong / and who do not / appease your heart / piously / with sacrifices / and great gifts.'" As Persephone rejoices at the prospect of reunion with her mother, Hades slips her a pomegranate seed to eat to insure her return to the land of the dead.[11]

Demeter's encrusted blackness has softened, become pliable and indeed sacred, and this sense of her yielding accompanies Hades' statement to Persephone which indicates that his compulsive thrusts, libidinal lusts, and rampant seizures have somewhat cooled off, dried out, become more affairs of the heart. Hades is imaging his desire here. No longer blind in his compulsive desire, he is spinning fantasies about their potential mating. His imagining is containing his desire in a way that fixes it, marries it, slows it, making it more solid, firmer.

Simultaneously, the tyrannies are being tamed, reckoned with: Demeter's concealment is accompanied by Persephone's containment of pomegranate seed. As Goddess Demeter conceals the white seed in the upperearth, Persephone takes in the red-purple seed, necessitating a perennial return and attachment to the underworld as its queen.

Demeter's human, black rigidities have loosened and flowed into the ensouled mysteries. She has yielded to her inner sacred nature, loosened her heart's humor, lowered child into immortal fires permeating to the depths of the imagination germinating below. But she is still cold; she moves within her own territory, has not handed herself over. Simultaneously, the redness of Hades' fiery seizures has solidified. No longer is he searing and causing frenetic and hyperactive reactions. Now the redness is digested and thereupon slowly beckons a slow return, an embodiment of the very mysteries which Demeter in her concealment has penetrated.

Therapeutically, this relates to finding the image beneath each one of the starving woman's desires and compulsions. All excesses—food restrictions and obsessions, stealing seizures, domestic and other hyperactivities—have to be imaged. Who is lurking behind each seizure? What does the figure look like? What is the message in the demand? Red force was too sticky; it possessed her too readily. This possession showed up in the way starving woman continually reflected others and, like a blank screen, became them and in the way she was so attached to the compulsions. She has to swallow the red seed, incorporate it, hold it within her. Therapeutically, this means her exercising active imagination on red living forces, realizing the fiery imaginal shapes as forms of soul.

Red Wall of Flame Transforms Itself

Demeter greets her daughter with supreme joy and tells her that eating underworld food means returning to Hades for one third of the seasons, spending the other two with her above.

Slowly her heart stops grieving, and mother and daughter give and receive joy from each other. Hecate then appears to them in a bright headband, and from that day onward she is constant companion to Persephone. Rhea then comes to Demeter, repeating the judgment that Persephone will spend a third of the year in the underworld and the remainder with her mother. They discuss this on the Rarion field, fertile in the past but no longer productive, having concealed the white barley according to Demeter's rule. Rhea asks Demeter to make the crops productive for humans.

The conjunction of Hades' realm with Demeter's is expressed by the fruition of the Rarion field. Demeter immediately brings forth a harvest: the entire earth blossoms, and Rarion itself produces ripe ears of corn. Demeter then reveals to the Eleusinian people her mysteries "which are impossible / to transgress / or to pry into, / or to divulge / for so great / is one's awe / of the gods / that it stops the tongue." And when Demeter has accomplished all this, they go to Olympus to remain in the company of the other gods and goddesses.[12]

The fertility of Rarion occurs only when Persephone's journey to and from Mother is woven into the fabric of all living things. The red seed, concealed and digested by the female, can blossom, become the harvest, when mother and daughter are in conjunction.

The image of Mother entering the underworld through her seed shows another consciousness entering into the woman. Whose consciousness is this? Who all along has understood Mother's destructive aspect and has seen that Persephone and Demeter are not opposed? We have come across her throughout: Hecate of the crescent moon, companion of Demeter and Persephone, lady of the crossroads, messenger of the soul.[13] Hecate's light assisted Demeter in locating the lost daughter, and it is present in the joyous reunion. Hecate bears Gaia's ancient ability to have simultaneous access to matter and image, upper- and underworlds, Mother connected to the erotic pulse underlying and permeating all material things. Hecate has understood all along that skeletal woman has emanated from the realm of essence, transforming and allowing the material world to shimmer, fully animated. Hecate knows to follow, not to force-feed her.

It is difficult for the starving woman to gain perspective toward her own brittle hardness and inner tyranny, to find an imaginal (Hecatean), rather than literal, perspective toward her desires. One example of this struggle is a bulimic woman, Helen, who would vomit after large meals compulsively gorged and watch everything she ate. Also, she kept finding herself in tyrannizing situations with powerfully dynamic and controlling men: cold, jealous, emotionally closed lovers as well as seductive and manipulative coworkers. The following portion of a dream occurred within the context (in the dream) of being in New York City at an all-day seminar in Feeding Ourselves (an organization for anorexia and eating disorders) which this woman actually attended. Thomas is a colleague she was then fighting through affirmative action because of his controlling and seductive advances while on the job. The dream portion:

> After being in a Feeding Ourselves seminar all day, I went out into a bar/cafe, saw some members of my team (at work), Penny and Alice, so I went over to the empty chair next to Alice to try to make peace (because of Thomas) and as I sat, looked up; Thomas was sitting next to Penny and across from Alice. He glared at me and said hello how was I. I glared back and wanted to leave. My girl friend Susan came to the table. I got up to walk her out, asking her if she used the Al Jarreau tickets I sent her. I then went to go find my shoes in the other building. I went back to the bar and a male friend introduced me to a friend of his. I sat down next to the latter in a love seat, he sat right next to me. I made a comment about how much room he was giving me and I got up to leave. I was then in a hospital with a man. We were given a baby to watch while the nurse was on break. The baby had trouble breathing. She was laid upside down in the carriage. She still had problems breathing so he picked her up and fed her. She was having serious problems. So I took the baby and patted her on the back. No success, so we found a nurse who got on the intercom and

called a doctor saying emergency, a baby had stopped breathing. I was feeling very responsible because we fed her. The doctor finally came. We then went walking. It was cold and snowing. The guy said to make the cold fun. So he put a pair of skis on me and I skied down the hill laughing and falling. Then he took the skis up the incline to try it.

The dream suggests that when Helen attempts to rectify (in a sense, to whitewash) the Thomas affair he comes face to face with her, glaring. She cannot escape him; he wants dialogue with her. A glare is a fierce or angry stare represented by a strong, dazzling light (brilliant reflection) as from sunlight on ice. Glaring has a spark connoting coldness and hardness. Thomas's glare reflects her own ("He glared at me and said hello how was I. I glared back and wanted to leave."); she is attempting here to leave both glares, losing the spark as well as the ice edge. In the cold and hard place of *both* being in the Thomas glare and wanting to get away from it (the defense against her own glare), there are accompanying aspects:

(a) "My girl friend Susan came to the table. I got up to walk her out, asking her if she used the Al Jarreau tickets I sent her. I then went to go find my shoes in the other building."

Helen describes Susan as quite a bubbly, social person. Susan comes up, and Helen walks away with this very extraverted, giggly friend, discussing the tickets she gave her. Helen tries to overlook, soften up, overgenerously wrap up the Thomas glare by this friendly expression of one-sided gift-giving. To leave the glare, she gives out to (that is, supports) the chatty, superficial aspects. Evidently, underlying Helen's talkativeness and social extraversion lies a glare which is avoided, discarded, and which seeks attention. The dream tells us to see through Helen's bubbly exterior side and to locate the glare waiting within. Also, we see that her conviviality and giving occur without shoes; they are not grounded; her feet are exposed, light, not grounded.

(b) "I went back to the bar and a male friend introduced me to a friend of his. I sat down next to the latter in a love seat, he sat right next to me. I made a comment about how much room he was giving me and I got up to leave."

She "acts out" the cold. Projecting warmth onto a stranger, she displaces the cold onto him. When she is in the place of the Thomas glare, she hands out her coldness and hardness, cannot sit with it. A love seat is the place of holding and containing emotional feelings without sexual acting-out, a place to sit side by side in a way which precludes symbiotic merging or defensive distancing. It is hard to sit with a stranger in the place of the Thomas glare. Afraid of being closed in, overwhelmed, she leaves with a sarcastic bite and an accusation not quite warranted. The coldness is put on as a way to protect herself when she cannot hold her own seat, stay grounded; the coldness appears displaced, an "acting-out" which does not serve her. If the stranger *were* too indulgent on the love seat, and if the cold were more an inherent part of her nature, her bite would make *him* get up.

(c) "I was then in a hospital with a man. We were given a baby to watch while the nurse was on break. The baby had trouble breathing. She was laid upside down in the carriage. She still had problems breathing so he picked her up and fed her. She was having serious problems. So I took the baby and patted her on the back."

Helen participates in feeding a baby who has trouble breathing. The connection between lungs and soul, lungs and the "disease of love," is documented by Homer and in modern form by Onians.[14] The dream tells us here how Helen uses *material solutions* for difficulties in soul and love. She acts materially to solve immaterial and essential difficulties. So to face the glare would entail living within the soul's blockage instead of attempting to solve it all in material terms; to avoid the glare, she stuffs food down. She uses the literal food and physical contact (patting) to obstruct and terminate the soul disease instead of meeting the breathing on its own level.

(d) "No success, so we found a nurse who got on the intercom and called a doctor saying emergency, a baby had stopped breathing. I was feeling very responsible because we fed her. The doctor finally came."

There is no nurse in sight (they are given the baby when the nurse is on a break); she has not been able to take the nurse stance (that is, of using a more intuitive, psychic, even rhythmic and instinctual, connection to the baby). Rather than submitting to and trusting her own nurturant instincts, she calls upon the nurse to summon a doctor: another material and external solution for the breathing problem. She goes to the ultimate authority instead of nursing through her breath. (Demeter's sweet breath which nourishes Demophoön is not present.)[15]

(e) "We then went walking. It was cold and snowing. The guy said to make the cold fun. So he put a pair of skis on me and I skied down the hill laughing and falling. Then he took the skis up the incline to try it."

Her fifth evasion of the glare is to transform the cold into fun.[16] The one who makes the cold fun for her is also the one who fed the baby. The snow is too soft and fluffy; the ripple of laughter is too forced. Again, we find external giggles covering the granular edge.

For reasons only great Gaia can know, Helen is asked in the Thomas affair to face and encounter a brutally glaring and harsh figure of soul. So we see Helen's difficulty in meeting the glare and allowing it to *transform itself.* The time she does encounter the ice within the glare, she either uses the cold (to get off the love seat) or changes it to a white pouf. The edge is gone; the snow is not icy or granular. They romp. So it all goes back to beginnings, symbiosis with earth mother, the children stuffed inside Gaia's huge belly. Demonic Thomas with glare therefore must wait until he can reemerge through symptoms.

Meanwhile, Helen does resort to her basic solution of starve-gorge–vomit cycles; this is her way of enacting the Thomas compulsions as well as her literal resistance to letting in any of these messages of soul. Therapeutically, as the Demeter-Persephone mytheme illustrates, the attempt would be to help the woman know Hecate as nurse of soul, the one who yields to meet the breathing problem more on its own level, taking in the image within each of her material solutions, isolating the coldness within the glare, allowing it to educate, to produce and transform on its own. In this way psychic figures can finally be severed from their exclusive and bodily possession.

This opening of starving woman's inner eye and ear to the imaginal landscape is difficult, of course, because of her continual literalization with food. She wants to act out, become the cold and brittle skeleton, locate it all compulsively in body; from that stance images must appear intangible, nonsensical. Even for the once imaginative ones, the early years of poetry and personifying have become camouflaged and entrapped by the black-red disease which keeps her acting out and obsessing with food.

What helps in this process is to give the woman a seat on silver-fleece, like Iambe with Doso–Demeter, a place to stay close to and feel the wound in isolation, the well of her sorrow. This takes patience and a desire to follow, like Hecate. For a long while, Helen, in therapy with me and beginning to open to an imaginal reality, only saw gray—a dull, gray fog on a damp earth, one isolated tree in sight, no sounds, smells, no one there. We stayed with that gray fog for about one month. Nothing moved; we were patient. Occasionally, there would be an accompanying image of a little stick man who would sit on top of her head, at times venturing down to her stomach with her. There would be tears as she described what they saw there: hands clutching, grasping, and pulling at her stomach. There were no sounds or voices, but the tears were the beginning of a moistening and loosening, a first speaking of a rusty heart.

Meanwhile, dream analysis continued, including the dream previously discussed, and we would read the events of her life imagistically as dream, opening up to the perspective where each event began to resound with metaphorical significance[17] (burning the child).

Eventually, the flint sickle was struck, and the spark appeared when to one session she carried hate and frustration.

One other compulsive scenario, one other cut-off relationship, and this was *felt*, not whitewashed. This place of hate and frustration was that which she said ordinarily preceded the gorging–starving cycle and which that cycle temporarily appeased.

Asked what she saw with an inner eye (severing herself from adhesion to dayworld events), she said, "a wall of red." It was there to block her; she wanted "to get through it" or "do something with it." This (I suggest) is what makes it want to block her; let it do whatever it is doing. She says that it will not move for her; she is very angry. I suggest the wall is no more stiff or stubborn than she is being toward it and that she let it do whatever it is doing. The following piece of "active imagination" ensued:[18]

> The red wall now is topped with flames which are active and moving. I now see myself on top of them and they are carrying me like water. These flames are carrying me to a "focal point," a distant point. They carry me to a big stone castle which is cold and damp and sturdy. It is a fortress, a beautiful, isolated place with a moat around it. I am inside now, the floor is cold and moist, it is completely empty with a gray-green mold on all the stone. I am standing under an archway which is overlooking a gray overpass leading to another part of the castle. Next to me is a short walkway that I can look over and I see a steep drop with rocks and scrubby trees. I walk down the walkway to the main part of the castle, and go up the four steps into the building which takes me to a huge open room of stone, empty yet beautiful. It contains a fireplace which is dark, not in use. The entire room is dark, damp. On the other side of the room is a staircase going up—I ascend and stand on the balcony, looking down, leaning on the railing, staring at the fireplace, and the stone of the room. The early frustration is gone, I feel calmer now. I wait like this for a while. Then I begin to imagine the room full of people with tuxedos and huge ballroom gowns dancing to baroque music, I hear a harpsichord playing, there is much food and drink. I am wearing a very full white satin gown and white satin shoes, but I am not with anyone. I descend the staircase and dance with several men. Two in particular stand out. One has very dark hair and a dark

mustache, he is tall with dark eyes, a white shirt under a dark tuxedo; he has large hands, good stature, his name is Philip. The other man has dirty blond hair, is shorter with very large shoulders, is dressed in a lighter white tuxedo. He is Andrew; has blue eyes and fair skin. Philip is a bit sharp and cool and formal yet interesting. He is not at ease, is quite concise, chooses his words carefully, does not laugh much or tell jokes, mainly discusses his travels. Andrew is warm and smiling, mostly he laughs and tells jokes, is very entertaining and charming, easy to be with; we "dance up a storm." A woman friend of mine, Sharon, is there wearing a darker dress than mine. We can share without speaking. Sharon dances with Philip while I dance with Andrew. We are all too busy to eat. Andrew is telling me funny stories about his life, we are laughing.

A first impulse is to do something with the red. When it is most in possession of us, when it tosses and hurls us in our fits of compulsion, turmoil, and hate, we most want to do something with it or in some way get through it (instead of see through it or allow it to form itself). This adds to the frustration and turns self-destructive. Demeter's resistance to the fires of the underworld accompanied her own paralysis and self-destructive blackness until she withdrew and yielded to Iambe/ Baubo's underworld humor. This woman, too, must withdraw from the literal, external world events, yield to the redness, face it in a way which lets it transform itself and educate her.

Coexisting as a part of the moving flames is the cold and sturdy castle. Somehow, facing the red leads to closing oneself off in the sturdy fortress of dampness. There is much stone in this place, stone which breeds only mold, steep drops, and scrubby trees; the fireplace is dark. Indeed, this moment is the core of *nox profunda*: Demeter by the well, the damp, cold, vacuous place, the chasm feared by every woman who uses literal food to fill it. Instead of scurrying from this place, the woman now pauses. She stays within the depths of her cold fortress, and within the cool and hollow dampness there is calm. She is above yet a part of and face to face with the fireplace and the stone of the room. She is perfectly still in a way which allows an inner light to expand and fill the room. Demeter laughs, sips the barley drink lightly touched with mint; she is holding Demophoön in flame. After holding the fire-child, she ignites into sacred beauty and, entempled, has seed within. The woman is standing on the balcony, staring at the cold fireplace and the stone of the room. Within this stare, a burst of images embodies itself: the fire shines in its hearth heating the elegant dancers, colors swirl to the delicate strains of the harpsichord accompanying the descent of her white satin gown.

Perhaps this is her "descending motion that announces a new vision of things," a "moment, in Corbin's language of *ta'wil*, that shift in mind enabling us to experience the sensate world of perception by means of the imaginal world."[19] She is beginning now to see things "first through a silvered imagining, an exegesis of events that leads them out of their physical encasement."[20]

Smooth white satin brings forth new (yet old) dancing partners. We have a dark, formal man and a laughing, lighter one. Therapeutically, at this point we are cautious. What will prevent this white satin ballroom dance from whitewashing the castle's damp mold and stone hardness? What prevents Andrew's laughter from turning snow to downy fluff? But if we look closely, the glimmer has its own hard edge, and this white satin has its own shadows, allowing the images a body with a rub that will move the woman, not merely be used by her.

We see that Andrew's humor contains a certain seduction and accompanies Philip's concise and meticulous choice of words, formality and sharpness, as well as the speech within the silence of the dark woman companion. All this preserves the edge. And all these qualities need careful and active psychic exchange.[21] One must keep that fire in the fireplace going; the therapist has to turn up the heat to continue dancing with them into the night. Woman needs to hold on to the presences of Philip, Andrew, and the dark woman friend, keep them around her, hear what they say, see what they move.

Goddess Demeter sits in the temple, white seed concealed in the ground. Within the movement of the dance, the woman is held still enough that the concealed seed begins germinating. When she familiarizes herself with Andrew and Philip, "walks on their heads and shoulders,"[22] she is releasing herself by lowering and loosening to the imaginal world. It is to this that her compulsions and restrictive defenses have beckoned her.

A Hecatean perspective, Hecate as nurse, here means assisting the woman in staying close to the void (damp fortress) and remaining within it as temple of the shades. A Hecatean consciousness would shed light on the figures so the woman could know them through her heart instead of identifying so concretely with them[23] or acting them out in repetitious scenarios with actual people. It means letting those "inner voices" speak, giving them form, placing them, becoming related to them. Each figure comes with his or her own demands and requests. The woman will have to find ways of bringing them up into the world, embodying their desires. Time for Philip's coldness to be faced and danced with: this the only way to the cool psychic depths where we become companion to the psychic beauty of the spouse of Red Hades, Persephone herself, Queen of Destruction.

Chapter VIII
Daimon Ice Woman w/ Bitch

We recall that Ellen West was beckoned by specific mysterious figures. Had she been educated to cultivate an imaginal perspective, to go through the underworld terrain which summoned her, she could have given birth to and become nurse of Sea-King, God-Father, Glorious Woman, and Armed Man, too. This process would have entailed Binswanger's assistance in the delineation of these psychic figures, allowing their full texture and voice to unfold, exploring their relation to her, what they sought from her. When they were not distant enough to inspire her through what became her poetry, they overwhelmed her and manifested themselves in her compulsive greed for and inhibition around food.[1]

Ellen knew the figures and voices mainly as evil and demonic spirits; we wonder how they might have served her more as guardian angels, daimones.[2] Had she yielded to the messages of those figures, she might have found enough distance from them to have begun to see their various presences in her daily actions. Therapeutically, this distance relates to delineation: personifying and eventually engaging in forms of "active imagination." It entails dialoguing with these figures, taking in their vengeances, their solace, hating them, loving them, giving them her desires, dreams, fears, and (mostly) compulsions.

Ellen too quickly moved out of her *longing* (beckoning her to the place of psychic presences) into *hunger* (for literal food).[3] Instead of gobbling or fleeing the sweets, the woman must stop; in order to build a temple for daimones, she must cut herself from, slice her greed from, the external food by sitting down and fully feeling the longing. She must sit within the greed. In the chasm of her own ravenous and bottomless pit, she can begin to see the images pulsating through her ardent desires. She begins to feel and sense, even dance with, the autonomous psychic figures of her desiring heart.

Interpreting, explaining, and observing the imaginal figures are not the way; the figures of soul do not respond to our mental constraints. Observing is not the same as facing; explaining is not the same as dancing. Reductive classification is not the issue; naming is. Demeter names herself as she founds her temple. Letting the figures name themselves is the point at which this woman, so sensitive to the psyche of others, begins a self-naming.[4]

Ellen West never was able to see that the psychic figures *were* her food, metaphorical food, the seed concealed. All her control and desire remained attached to external food, and this attachment drained her imaginal fertility. The only way the starving woman can work out of her compulsive–inhibitive relation to food is through an education on how to work with the imaginal as it presents itself to her through food.

Such therapeutic work absolves the psychic figures from having to become literalized through symptoms or personal relations (with mother, male, or therapist). Specifically, such personifying releases the woman from entanglement with the personal mother, to whom she has had to cling to remember the desires of the original Mother. This psychic engagement gives both starving woman and personal mother a breath of fresh air and allows the distance doctors have been trying to obtain through literal isolation.[5]

Her being driven by and for food everywhere, along with driving the body in inexorable ways, her relying upon endless charts and diets and scales coupled with her infinite gorging and vomiting show that the female, too, has a 'fire,' a combustible aspect which the alchemists spoke of as sulfur.[6] Found abundantly in volcanic regions, this substance, also known as brimstone, represents the spirit of fire.[7] Female is living out the underworld flames dramatically and self-destructively in her most familiar room of the house: the kitchen.

At least within this pathology of food, we see the attempt by the woman to struggle with the sulfuric side, the redness of her most passionate nature. In past centuries she has lived it out vicariously through the man's escapades or as a deviant crossing over to the male ways of sparking the combustion. This food pathology represents the female struggle with sulfur in a landscape which is our own: our food, body, and reproduction. Raging sulfur possesses the starving woman to the bitter end or until the blossoming of an underworld perspective turns it around.

What is being worked out here is the female's awakening to her own sulfuric potency and the necessity of allowing it the distance to shape and form itself creatively: her sulfur—desires, vitalities, burnings—"the force that through the green fuse drives the flower"[8]—her glare. This is what Mother asks her to place. We assist this placing and naming of the sulfuric side by allowing the woman the distance to sit alone and let the redness take shape while feeling its desires, as with Helen's red wall. This pause ceases the dramatic, compulsive enactment of the sulfuric aspect[9] in terms of food and body, and we begin to explore the sulfur as image.

To engage the sulfur imaginally means returning to where food is "alive" and potentially poisonous and dangerous. Remember that the invisible animation of food moves her, feeds her, drives her. Food carries the tyrant, the psychic presence which is destructive, death-dealing. The presences appearing within and through food need to be digested, not vomited.

So we allow the food to be alive, to return to the living: matter as animated, food ensouled. We allow the food to glare out its poisonous forces. Who is taking shape? Red man? Leopard? Bossman? Armed man? How does starving woman relate to this figure? It is interesting, if not disconcerting, to see how often this sulfuric side of power and vitality is represented in male form (even for woman-identified women who have changed culturally their gender allegiance). Since external men have enacted sulfuric aspects for thousands of years—and cultivated this particularly through sports, war, government—it is not surprising that, in the reservoirs of our memories, sulfur is imaged as male. As we open ourselves to the panorama of the female imagination, we can relate to sulfur in ways compatible with our inherent nature[10] (Red Hades to pomegranate seed within).

The therapeutic process involves delineation of the fire-figure exacting vengeance through food. We must name it, find out its texture and context. Also, we must be aware of the tendency to meddle with human concerns. When Demeter was beginning to engage with what was becoming an immortal fire-spirit, a daimon-of-sulfur, Metanira interfered with dayworld and personal fears.

This interference reminds us how easy it is to identify the awakening fire-aspect as male and live it out too personally and subjectively in emotional terms (serving an actual male tyrant, for example; or, therapeutically, working exclusively on such relationships). Leaving one's ground to know sulfur in its common manifestations is not the way to the potency of our hot inner nature. Instead, woman is consumed; there is no body, no hearth to contain and craft the flame. It leads to disembodied ambitions or tyrannical compulsions.

Demeter kept her own ground, insisted on her own grain drink, as she engaged with fire-spirit. As therapists we have to remember that a temple must be built for one who is opening to inner psychic presence and particularly to sulfuric sides. Sulfur is found in the world and in all living things,[11] and it returns itself to the world far too fast, without containment, digestion.[12] It fires us up as we attach ourselves to the object of our desire.

Sulfur beckons and possesses the woman with her obsessions and compulsions around literal food. Her desires and fires all become attached to food (and thereby lost to her). Her incessant desire to *have* the food has been all that lit up the world for her, preventing her from knowing the spark of that which makes the food desirable.

Demeter is in her temple as Hades and Persephone 'marry.' Persephone digests the red seed giving her rule over the underworld. Swallowing the seed shows that Persephone has her own red sulfur, her hot inner nature. The digestion guarantees against her consumption by 'external' fiery tyrannies; it shows she can contain the red and not be possessed by it. She can carry it up and out to Mother's terrain—and return. Female has to 'marry' the sulfur by digesting it, containing it within so it circulates interiorly through blood and heart; then she can engage it in and through the world.

Such digestion entails enough distance from and delineation of the red to swallow it. What facilitates this distance and delineation, this containment of red seed, is Sweet Sound and Hate.[13]

Many starving patients are described by the clinicians and physicians as hearing inner voices. Not all these voices are demanding or denigrating; some are melodic, soothing, exquisite. We imagine that Ellen's Glorious Woman had a sweet, alluring voice. Such sounds carry the woman to soul-companions who can assist her journey through an underworld that need not be Hell.

The sirens with lyre and double flute were companions and servants of the Goddess of the Underworld. They would seduce travelers to Persephone by "the sweet tones of their music and song."[14] Such sounds are not sweet in the sense of being innocent; they do not defend against underworld realities. They are enticing ways to be beckoned to an underworld perspective; if the woman opens herself to the "sounds of her inner ear" (Helen's harpsichord), perhaps there will be melodic incantations she can follow.

Sweet tones of psyche can carry her messages which, when personified, become the guardian angels of soul. The guidance of such figures will give her company in the unfolding of an imaginal perspective. Lyre and flute were the favorite instruments of Sappho. Through her mixolydian mode, she would invite women to unfold their shimmering Aphroditic beauty.[15] Woman has an alluring anima also, a dear companion assisting her in knowing the soul's journey through her most exquisite aesthetic sensibilities.

Perhaps, also, the sweet tones resonate with the inner pulse, and she can dance. She will move and bend and yield to the soul-companions, find the mistresses of soul in her body's motions. Their loving messages of how soul animates all worldly things remind us that the "hidden waves"[16] lying within and beyond each bodily event are also sound waves. They pulsate. Subtle scales of lyre and flute arouse the passions, too, and truly are prayers to Aphrodite. The sweet sounds of love's seductions carry the starving woman to the bittersweet mysteries underlying dayworld necessities. This fall into love when one is struggling with sulfur ultimately brings forth the redness and fire, carrying her again and again to hate.

On digesting the red seed, Persephone, no longer innocent maiden, becomes Goddess of the Dead, Queen of Destruction. The river Styx (associated with the Greek verb meaning "to hate") nine times circles her underworld. The Goddess Styx became the offspring of Zeus and Persephone.[17] The spirits of revenge, the Erinyes, "Three hellish Furies, boltered all with blood;/Their form and bearing were made woman-wise; / Vivid green hydras girt them, and a brood / Of asps and adders, each a living tress, / Writhed round the brows of that fell sisterhood,"[18] were in the Orphic tales offspring of Hades and Persephone.[19] Persephone sends the petrifying head of Medusa to the gates of the underworld, turning invaders to stone: "this head is, in a sort, the other aspect of the beautiful Persephone."[20]

Hate has run through the entire mytheme. Gaia's hate and revenge created the crescent sickle which broke the gods out of their material entrapment. Demeter's fury cooled into "icefall isolation"[21] and temple longing, rage becoming hate. At first her rage was too personal, red sulfur raging through the blackened bitternesses; but then came the loosening and moistening with humor and barley drink, a cooling, silver pause. She then had the coolness to let go of the child as personal, becoming impersonal mother of flame-spirit, and the rage cooled to a hate of the temple, a purer, more sacred form of hate with an effect even over Almighty Zeus.

Hate is often the means by which we see poignantly and clearly with an inner eye, have insight which penetrates to the Gods in all worldly things (Helen's Red Wall). Hate's glare cuts through to rockbottom foundations. We often see those we hate in sharper focus than those we love. The hated one stalks us everywhere. For it is the one we hate the most who bears messages to us about sides of the psyche most denied, neglected. The hated one carries our most terrible lack.

To melt the brittle starving woman, go to hate. She has been hardened beyond the joys of puppy love; her way, even in what she knows as love, is hate. Hate is a whiter form of the redness of wrath or fury; it is cooler. Ice Woman with red seed pulsing through the body: the redness is there, stirring the entire being, yet is not lashed out, kept in an ice shield, and as it circulates it cools to hate. She faces the sulfur, the fat of her aching desire;[22] she does not act it out but knows it also within as it permeates every living thing. Sulfur charges her body; her skin stands on edge, prickles with the cold of a hate which keeps off touch while the redness in its circulation images itself to her, a type of dance.

If well worked, hate is a way to move like Persephone to and from the black rigidities and fixities (I can't move, I'm trapped,

I feel lost, life is empty) to the red fires (I can't control the eating, I can't stop vomiting, I have to work harder, I can't get food or that bastard off my mind), staying psychologically cool yet mobile.

The psychological hate of Persephone is not directed out or in. It is not the ferocious form of redhot fury which vents itself in destruction, nor is it the black sulkiness of passive withdrawals. To swallow and digest the red seed entails facing that ninth circle of hell with the ice woman whose eyes petrify. When the focus is removed from food or literal male tyrants with whom the starving woman is in emotional relation,[23] she has to face her ice woman, daimon of soul.

Sitting in one's own psychic cold stare is much more difficult than being or acting out of that coldness, or being driven compulsively to avoid it, or starving to warm up a tyrannical lover. Up to now, while possessed by red tyrant's compulsions, projecting her coldness, the starving woman has blindly and rather indiscriminately vented her antagonisms and sharp bite. Now perhaps she can come face to face with the red demons accompanying the cold and begin to discriminate them, which is to know herself.

This process entails looking at the food she most desires and allowing that desire to shape itself even when it emerges as the figure (tyrant of fat) she most hates.[24] Sitting within the desire leads us to the one most hated who asks for our engagement. Biting into the food now involves facing the red-eyed figure. She faces it, lets go, and imagistically engages with it. Invader gets turned to stone, mother-killers are swallowed, fat man is encircled: each move gives her more substance, carrying her down to the river's last circle, a descent which is a sort of submission occurring when dark Mother loosens to her own frailty and humor, allowing the emergence of piercing silver-blue eyes and sharp tongue, the beauty that fixates as it transforms, the Queen of Destruction herself. She is the one who sees the red as sensuous, independent body, faces it as mate, and also nurses it.

Demeter's final lowering occurred when she knew the red-spirit through nursing it, holding it in the fire as nurse. Sometimes the raging redness just asks to be impersonally handled by a nurse.

Now there is less need to adhere to the world's potencies and be tyrannized naively and blindly by them. Ice Woman has throbbing purple-red, bittersweet seed within, shining surface containing the crimson juice of paradox and mystery, now materialized and digested, serving as protective measure against the red villains and their possessive forms of consumption. If she cannot keep digesting the vital heat of red (imaging it through her worldly desires) and embodying it (creatively letting those images form themselves), it will be split off from her and literalized again in rampant desires and compulsions.

Since the ice is slippery, she no longer sticks to others' effusive emotions; the oily base of their desirous longings does not keep ground with her and no longer consumes. Instead, they slip off. She can attach and glide in the world with vitality, without losing herself in those attachments. Ice Woman helps starving woman let go of food's sticky pull. She does not give up food but digests the red carried in it which depotentiates its tyranny while charging her interior circulation and blood-pulse.

Ice Woman keeps the starving woman strong yet resilient, and this prevents her from so readily melting into the imaginal pool of another, from serving as Iris-medium only. Ice Woman has her own dazzling reflections, and the Hecatean barking bitches surrounding her keep off those who would use her as a blank screen only. She learns how to snap.

There is a difference between Iris and Hecate as messenger-goddesses. For a starving woman struggling with sulfur and getting to know the ice, Iris is dangerous. Demeter sends Iris back to Zeus; Iris does not belong in this mytheme. She would return it all to beginnings:[25] maiden Persephone romping in flowery fields and subject to the commands of a Father Zeus. Likewise, Iris would have her continue serving the Hades figure as a compliant maiden girl, a blatant denial of the inherent relation of the female to the sulfuric red.

Unlike Iris with her rainbows, Hecate is messenger in a bitchy sense: her message bares teeth, is conveyed with a snarl. Hecate allows intercourse with the world's sulfur with a bite which precludes consumption.[26] Hands off, she growls. She understands the connection between Demeter and Persephone: how daughter brings up her mysteries, lives in them, sees them through the world, always containing (digesting) the underworld fires while in the world. She knows this carrying-up of the underworld mysteries needs protection: the stickiness of sulfur's attraction asks for continual distancing.

So Hecate is a protective bitch, not a controlling one. The latter is only necessary when the woman is split from the underworld, has nothing to stand on, is in the void yet wants to remain blind to it, has lost her soul. Yet Hecate places certain steps on the invisible ground below. With the intelligent instincts of an undomesticated bitch, she knows her way in the dark, continually sniffing out the terrain as she circles the sulfur queen, keeping her within certain limits.

Slippery-cool Ice Woman accompanied by Bitch Hecate can work off the sulfur of the world. She is no maiden in an ivory tower separated from the world's flame. With hidden red seed and the lyre's sweet sounds, she is sensual in her coolness. She is as stubbornly firm as she is stubbornly tender and mobile. The flux of delicate images shimmers off her icy white contour. One senses diamonds in its shine. Always her ice suggests the momentum and force of the ice-waters running deep, rapids connecting her with the inner rhythm of the world's pulse, the desirous gaping of the world's mouth.

Therefore, she does not leave the world but rather enters and is moved by the colors, tastes, textures, and emotional tones all around, seeing them with a distance not of frozenness as much as the coolness of a "critically imagining eye." There is beauty in this distance as she resonates with the beauty of the world.[27] She tenderly can be enticed into the world's pulse, yet at the point of devouring there comes the knife-edge of cynical glances, the bitch bark, the slippery ice letting go, releasing by capturing it all as image.

This movement in the world is not in abstraction but comes with a bitch-animal immediacy keeping everything riding the whitewater rapids. A doctor examining her bends over too closely; a stranger sits on a love seat too near; now she can sense the spark while gazing over the man's shoulder to see the red sulfuric one laughing in the background. Connected to the image through heart and humor, she bites at the doctor-stranger with an artful retort, a snappy one-liner. He takes one step back, knowing the joke is not on him alone, that he has not to leave the room entirely; she has held her ground elegantly and is stirred vitally. She is laughing while dancing and dialoguing with the red one—a form of digestion.

The table offers her cakes, breads, jams, pastries. Her claw goes out, yet now she can see the opening jaws of red bossman riding lion, urging her to blind the imaginal eye and consume. She keeps the eye open (Hecate's headband shining),[28] sees him clearly: the jungle, the swish of the lion's tail. She takes one piece of pastry which carries and is surrounded by the green mysteries of that jungle. She watches the lush foliage unfold as she takes one bite. Images fill her, also. One pastry is enough. She leaves the table. Each of Hecate's bites has substance, a vital world in itself.

Hecate as the bitch-whore allows this intercourse with the world's sulfur, and for the starving woman this pertains mainly to food. Food is the language of this pathology attempting to re-connect the female with her (lost) underworld components, so of course it cannot be ignored. Imaginal work does not preclude the things of the world. One cannot work with psychic figures to the exclusion of attending to food, nor can one 'make' the woman, with imaginal eye opened, resume a 'normal diet.' Therapy directed to a Hecatean perspective will help the woman open her eye to soul, seeing the metaphor in all food.

After all, eating in the underworld gave Persephone a way back to Demeter. Food can germinate an awakening to psychological 'death,' to an imaginal consciousness. This was the lesson of the Eleusinian initiates who fasted and drank potions to prepare for the vision of (in a sense transformation to) Persephone holding the ear of wheat, which allowed them to see the shades of the dead existing in all living things.[29]

Therefore, the woman would go to soul—use her imagining eye—*through* body and food instead of at their expense. Hecate shows her she has been blessed with an underworld understanding of food. She has been graced with an understanding that what looks to the upperworld like garbage is in the underworld a sacrifice to the Gods. She will become aware of the connection of her eating with the autonomous psychic figures, come to see images as independent, sensuous, concrete morsels and the "sensible nature of the imagination."[30]

For example, the woman would become aware of the precision of her choices, how particular qualities of food—texture, sweetness, color, consistency—open her to specific psychic presences. She will become aware of her discriminations, that some substances feed certain psychic figures more than others.

At one time, Ellen West's "bizarre" diet was several pounds of tomatoes and twenty oranges daily.[31] The woman within a Hecatean perspective attends to such desire, tries to understand it metaphorically and asks: Whose fire is she feeding with all that red-orange substance?

This means watching the desire as it appears and seeing with what particular shape it defines itself. No restrictions or prohibitive measures are necessary; we just feel the desire while seeing with the "imagining eye" (Hecate's shining headband) what unfolds—sulfur no longer only in food as object-of-desire which must be grasped to be known, but sulfur shimmering out at us from the world's delight, sensually inviting us to an intercourse with the world. We gape, not grasp. Gaia's desire is in her gaping; Persephone's grasp[32] led to the rapacious descent to the underworld. What she had to learn in the journey was

Gaia's gaping as ground of it all. Persephone learned that the beauty shining forth from the flower was her own (narcissus). There was no need to grasp it; instead, she could stand in awe of the world's dazzling animation. Gaping sends us sensually to the underworld. What occurs when we take in the splendor of the world's sulfuric tinge is not an intimacy coming from subjective or personal dependency but one like Sappho knew, an intricate and exquisite rapport with the dew dazzling forth from all living things, a resonance with their sensuous nature.[33]

This intimacy entails seeing and sensing within the desire and imaginal intercourse with each morsel: Who is this feeding? What figure needs this sort of nourishment? Nurturing mother and sensual mistress are no longer dichotomous. The sensuality is found in the nourishment now. Once the woman knows intimately the imaginal figures, she attends to them, inquiring what *they* wish to be fed that day. If one in particular looms large and demands too much, perhaps she needs to give him/her/it something special to digest.[34]

This returns her to the sacredness of her food choices, how everything she digests connects her with presences larger than herself. Her sensuous relation with food now lies outside her subjective satiation/satisfaction. In this way, instead of being victim to the imaginal presence of each food morsel, she engages with it as in a dialogue with soul.

So food begins to take on aesthetic sensibilities; the woman is sensitized to an aesthetic perception within eating.[35] Seeing the images in each concrete morsel lets her be more engaged with the food; now she can *taste* it, make finer, more exquisite, sensual discriminations. Her desire is stimulated and, now danced with, does not consume her; she digests.

Different foods sound different to her; sirens call her to the beauty of specific foods. Such an aesthetic perception allows the woman to sense how spices, exotic and rich foods, as well as specific qualities of basic foods, fill her and carry psychic value. This sensitivity will return her consciously to psychic essence, an appreciation of how such foods echo an exoticism and richness of soul. And because food delicacies remind us of the modesty of soul,[36] huge quantities are no longer necessary.

An aesthetic perception of food in terms of its psychic significance lets her take food out of an exclusively personal context; eating food becomes ceremonial[37]—Food Aesthetics.[38] She sees that paying attention to how qualities of food stir and feed the beauty of the imagination, alluring her to soul, is more nourishing than consuming quantities of vitamins and proteins.

The starving woman is serving Gaia by working the female out of her upperworld fixities. Gaia needs to break down the female body and its relation to food and fertility to help the woman find her relation to soul and death, to contain the fire and brimstone of her sulfuric potency. Gaia is showing that the female has seed, too, can germinate. When the woman is able to digest the red seed, she reclaims her "drives," her "creativity."

The food pathology of starving woman calls us to psychological transformation, to the presence of the Goddess of Death entering through Hecatean consciousness. We must welcome Dark Mother with her ice, her bark, her temple; we must encourage one another to participate with her. What are the implications of this consciousness entering our culture? The female recovers the active presence and potency in her knife, her bite, her seed. First, food and cooking take on a new significance, becoming ritual preparations for an entry to psyche. No longer the place of monotonous domestic drudgery, the kitchen becomes a room in the underworld. Not mother as servant but mother as celebrant to the voices and figures of death residing in food, initiating her child into the ceremonial revelry of the underworld, the festivity of the many psychic members of the family.

*

We know that Ice Woman's digested seed accompanied the fruition of the field of Rarion, the womb. Every starving woman has potential offspring, a craft, beneath the skeletal surface. Every starving woman contains aesthetic endeavor if she can feel fully the sulfuric edge, digest it and dance with it, allowing it to take shape.

Ice Woman with red seed appears when Demeter takes back her Aphroditic qualities. Mothering takes on a new sensuality. No longer are redhot lusts opposed to the purities of sweet maternity:[39] the red seed cooled, whitened, shoots up the green fuse and makes every endeavor of the female an aesthetic one with its own inherent order—every action and event fused, sparked, sulfur shimmering through it all. And the sulfur chooses the ice and bitch's bark to define and contain itself, with its own borders, requirements, dimensions; within its fortress she finds an inherent fruition.

Sparked by the animation of the world, she can bring the fruition out, whether in child-care, medical work, legal transactions, literature, mechanics—there is nurturing with an intimacy, a craft with a sounding in every event, an angel in each word.[40] She takes in each of her desires, sees each in its contour and graceful line, participates in its crafting, its exquisite revelation, the unfolding of the design of its patterning. With every slice of the knife, instrument's paring, she hears the lyre beckon her always to the Ice Woman of her heart's desire, sulfuric pulse germinating deeply in each of her cool bites.

Notes*

Chapter I: Mother and Oppositionalism

1. S. Freud, Lecture 33, "Femininity," in *New Introductory Lectures* (New York: Norton, 1964), particularly pp. 129, 131. See also S. Freud, "Some Psychological Consequences of the Anatomical Distinction Between the Sexes," in *The Standard Edition of the Complete Psychological Works of Sigmund Freud*, ed. James Strachey, 24 vols. (London: Hogarth Press, 1953–1974), 19: 243; see also "Female Sexuality," *Standard Edition*, vol. 21. Freud, in *Civilization and Its Discontents* (New York: Norton, 1961), pp. 50–51, states: "Furthermore, women soon come into opposition to civilization and display their retarding and restraining influence—those very women who, in the beginning, laid the foundations of civilization by the claims of their love. Women represent the interests of the family and of sexual life. The work of civilization has become increasingly the business of men, it confronts them with ever more difficult tasks and compels them to carry out instinctual sublimations of which women are little capable. Since a man does not have unlimited quantities of psychical energy at his disposal, he has to accomplish his tasks by making an expedient distribution of his libido. What he employs for cultural aims he to a great extent withdraws from women and sexual life."

2. Susan Griffin, *Woman and Nature* (New York: Harper Colophon, 1980); see especially pp. 37 ff., 138 ff. Shulamith Firestone, *The*

*All page numbers are listed in the order of their quoting.

Dialectic of Sex (New York: William Morrow & Co., 1972), pp. 41–71. Juliet Mitchell, *Psychoanalysis and Feminism* (New York: Random House, 1975). Phyllis Chesler, *Women and Madness* (New York: Hearst Co., 1972), especially pp. 79 ff. Naomi Goldenberg, *The Changing of the Gods* (Boston: Beacon Press, 1979), especially pp. 26–46.

3. S. Freud, *Civilization and Its Discontents*, p. 92: "The fateful question for the human species seems to me to be whether and to what extent their cultural development will succeed in mastering the disturbance of their communal life by the human instinct of aggression and self-destruction. It may be that in this respect precisely the present time deserves a special interest. Men have gained control over the forces of nature to such an extent that with their help they would have no difficulty in exterminating one another to the last man. . . . And now it is to be expected that the other of the two 'Heavenly Powers', eternal Eros, will make an effort to assert himself in the struggle with his equally immortal adversary."

4. For a provocative and poetic exploration of the female imagination, see Susan Griffin; and also Monique Wittig, *Les Guérillères*, trans. David LeVay (New York: Viking Press, 1971).

5. See Shulamith Firestone, pp. 15–31, on the myth of Emancipation and the diffusion of the female struggle to uncover her inherent potency.

6. Rilke's vision of this transition to femininity: "The girl and the woman, in their new, their own unfolding, will but in passing be imitators of masculine ways and repeaters of masculine professions. After the uncertainty of such transitions it will become apparent that women were only going through the profusion and the vicissitude of those (often ridiculous) disguises in order to cleanse their most characteristic nature of the distorting influences of the other sex. . . . some day there will be girls and women whose name will no longer signify merely an opposite of the masculine, but something in itself, something that makes one think, not of any complement and limit, but only of life and existence: the feminine human being" (Rilke, *Letters to a Young Poet*, quoted in Nor Hall, *The Moon and The Virgin* [New York: Harper & Row, 1980], pp. 153–54).

7. Mary Daly, *Gyn/Ecology* (Boston: Beacon Press, 1978); and Adrienne Rich, *The Dream of a Common Language* (New York: Norton, 1978), particularly "Natural Resources," pp. 60–67.

8. James Hillman, *The Dream and the Underworld* (New York: Harper Colophon, 1979), p. 81.

9. As I state in the preface, I use "underworld" as does archetypal psychology, to mean a perspective which sees that everything material and literal reverts back to a realm of imaginal configurations which are prior to (yet permeating) the visible and concrete. For an extended discussion of this pneumatic realm of shades or images (*skiai* or *eidolon*) beyond and prior to the physical world, refer to Hillman, *Dream and the Underworld*, particularly pp. 35-58.

10. Ibid., see pp. 44-45 for Dionysus/Hades discussion and first section in chapter 4, pp. 68-74, on barriers.

11. James Hillman, *The Myth of Analysis* (New York: Harper Colophon, 1978), p. 287.

12. Hillman, *Dream and the Underworld*, p. 57, and generally chapter 3.

13. See, for example, A. Crisp, "Clinical and Therapeutic Aspects of Anorexia Nervosa. A Study of Thirty Cases," *J. Psychom. Res.* 9 (1965): 67; as well as D. W. K. Kay and D. Leigh, "The Natural History, Treatment and Prognosis of Anorexia Nervosa, Based on a Study of 38 Patients," *J. Ment. Sci.* 100 (1952): 411. Also, researchers have debated over the types within anorexia nervosa: for example, the distinction between typical and atypical cases, in H. Bruch, "Anorexia Nervosa and Its Differential Diagnosis," *J. Nerv. Ment. Dis.* 141 (1966): 555; the distinction between primary and secondary syndromes, in A. King, "Primary and Secondary Anorexia Nervosa Syndromes," *Brit. J. Psychiat.* 109 (1963): 470, also discussed in P. Dally and J. Gomez, *Anorexia Nervosa* (William Heinemann Medical Books, Ltd., 1979), chapter 2; and typical versus atypical hysterical depressive and astenic types, in S. Theander, "Anorexia Nervosa. A Psychiatric Investigation of 94 Female Patients," *Acta Psychiatrica Scandinavica Supplementaum* 214 (1970). See also for an overall review of diagnostic issues: G. R. M. Russell, "Anorexia Nervosa: Its Identity as an Illness and Its Treatment," in *Modern Trends in Psychological Medicine,* ed. J. H. Price (Butterworth, Great Britain, 1970), pp. 131-64; Kelly M. Bemis, "Current Approaches to the Etiology and Treatment of Anorexia Nervosa," *Psych. Bulletin* 85 (1978): 593.

14. H. Thoma, *Anorexia Nervosa* (New York: International Universities Press, 1967).

15. Listed in order according to the respective medical mode:

J. Charcot, *Diseases of the Nervous System*, vol. 3 (London: The New Sydenham Society, 1889), pp. 210-14; W. W. Gull, "Anorexia Nervosa (Anorexia Hysteria)," *Clinical Sociological*, No. 7 (1874): 22-28. S. Silver, "'Simmond's' Disease (Cachexia Hypophyseopriva). Report of a Case with Postmortem Observations and Review of Literature," *Arch. Int. Med.* 51 (1933): 175; I. H. Pardee, "Cachexia Nervosa: A Psychoneurotic Simmond's Syndrome," *Arch. Neurol. & Psychiat.* 41 (1939): 841; R. Nicholson, "Simmond's Disease," *Lancet* 1 (1936): 951. J. R. Waller, M. R. Kaufman and F. Deutsch, "Anorexia Nervosa: A Psychosomatic Entity," *Psychosom. Med.* 2 (1940): 3; S. Lorand, "Anorexia Nervosa: Report of a Case," *Psychom. Med.* 5 (1943): 282; J. H. Masserman, "Psychodynamisms in Anorexia Nervosa and Neurotic Vomiting," *Psychoanaly. Quart.* 10 (1941): 211; B. C. Meyer and L. A. Weinroth, "Observations on Psychological Aspects of Anorexia Nervosa," *Psychosom. Med.* 19 (1957): 389; L. Linn, "Psychoanalytic Contribution to Psychosomatic Research," *Psychosom. Med.* 20 (1958): 88. I. C. Bernstein, "Anorexia Nervosa Treated Successfully with Electroshock Therapy and Subsequently Followed by Pregnancy," *Amer. J. of Psychiat.* 120 (1964): 1023; B. J. Blinder, D. M. A. Freeman and A. J. Stunkard, "Behavior Therapy of Anorexia Nervosa: Effectiveness of Activity as a Reinforcer of Weight Gain," *Amer. J. Psychiat.* 126 (1970): 77. G. K. Ushakov, "Anorexia Nervosa," in *Modern Perspectives in Adolescent Psychiatry*, ed. J. G. Howells (Edinburgh: Oliver & Boyd, 1971); Russell, "Anorexia Nervosa"; Dally and Gomez, *Anorexia Nervosa*.

16. Hillman anticipates and tries to avoid such simplifying in his *Re-Visioning Psychology* (New York: Harper Colophon, 1977); see pp. 57-58: "Here our intention is not to replace either the idea of illness or the idea of sin, nor to question the authenticity of medical and religious perceptions of the psyche. Our aim is to see them and see through them, as perspectives, while maintaining another view that differs from theirs and is psychological."

17. Hillman, *Dream and the Underworld*, p. 79.

18. H. Bruch, *Eating Disorders* (London: Routledge and Kegan Paul, 1973). Bruch here describes anorexia nervosa as "rare indeed, but the medical interest in it has always been great, quite out of proportion to its infrequent occurrence. The continual fascination with this rare condition is probably evoked by the tragedy of seeing a young person, in the bloom of youth, seeking solution to life's problems through this bizarre method of voluntary starvation, something that runs counter to all human experience" (p. 4). She continues that

she will be selective in her use of the literature, which she describes as representing a multitude of differing viewpoints (pp. 6–7). In a personal communication she showed me an Italian text which had over 1,000 references. Selvini's comprehensive text has approximately 730 references (Mara Selvini Palazzoli, *Self-Starvation* [London: Chaucer Publishing Co., 1974]).

Concerning the rarity of the disease which Bruch notes in 1973, it is interesting to see that in her recent text, *The Golden Cage: The Enigma of Anorexia Nervosa* (Cambridge: Harvard University Press, 1978), she discusses the rapidly increasing rate of anorexia in the last fifteen years and states, "Now it is so common that it represents a real problem in high schools and colleges. One might speak of an epidemic illness, only there is no contagious agent; the spread must be attributed to psychosociological factors" (p. viii).

19. See Hillman, *Re-Visioning Psychology*, p. 128.

20. Ibid., particularly pp. 74–75.

21. Thoma, p. 27.

22. Bruch, *The Golden Cage*, p. viii, states that ninety percent of anorexics are females; and Selvini, pp. 24–25, argues that the definition of anorexia nervosa should be reserved for the syndrome occurring in prepubescent and pubescent girls. Dally and Gomez include a chapter on factors relating to the low incidence in males. The following researchers also discuss how anorexia nervosa occurs in young adult females with male incidence only five to fifteen percent: E. L. Bliss and C. H. H. Branch, *Anorexia Nervosa; Its History, Psychology, and Biology* (New York: Paul Hoeber, 1960); Bruch, *Eating Disorders*; Crisp; and Theander. Also see Kim Chernin's discussion on the lack of serious *attention* to the relationship of food pathology to being female, *The Obsession: Reflections on the Tyranny of Slenderness* (New York: Harper & Row, 1981), pp. 62 ff. This is an excellent and penetrating study of the relation of weight disorders to female inferiority issues within the culture.

23. R. Morton, *Phthisiologia—or a Treatise of Consumptions* (London: Smith & Walford, 1694), discussed in Bliss and Branch. Selvini, in her historical survey, states that Morton is credited with the first detailed description of the disorder. Morton used the term "nervous atrophy" as the form of consumption which accompanied the chief characteristics of the disease: amenorrhea, lack of appetite, extreme emaciation (p. 4).

24. W. W. Gull, "Anorexia Nervosa" (1874), and "Anorexia Nervosa," *Lancet* 1 (1888): 516. See also E. D. Lasegue, "On Hysterical Anorexia," *Med. Times Gazette* 2 (1873): 265, in M. R. Kaufman and M. E. Heiman, *Evolution of Psychosomatic Concepts. Anorexia Nervosa: A Paradigm* (New York: International Universities Press, 1964).

25. P. Dubois, *The Psychic Treatment of Nervous Disorders* (New York: Funk & Wagnall, 1909), quoted in Kaufman and Heiman, p. 160.

26. These clinical aspects are amazingly consistent in the research, even between antithetical approaches and disciplines. For thorough descriptions, see Thoma; Selvini; Dally and Gomez; Ushakov; Bruch, *Eating Disorders*; Bruch, *The Golden Cage*.

27. Unless otherwise indicated, by "death" I mean metaphorical death, the psychological view that "death" means opening oneself to and honoring the underworld. See Hillman, *Dream and the Underworld*, pp. 64–67.

28. L. Binswanger, "The Case of Ellen West," in *Existence*, ed. R. May, E. Angel, and H. F. Ellenberger (New York: Simon & Schuster, 1958), p. 248.

29. Ibid., p. 295.

30. Ibid., pp. 278, 280, 295. It is also interesting to note here the connection with Persephone, Goddess of the Underworld, who "exemplifies the Greek idea of *non-being*" which "forms the root-aspect of being" (C. G. Jung and C. Kerényi, *Essays on a Science of Mythology*, trans. R. F. C. Hull, Bollingen Series XXII [Princeton: Princeton University Press, 1973], p. 120).

31. Ibid., pp. 244–45, 284.

32. Selvini, p. 25.

33. Dally and Gomez, p. 106.

34. Lasegue, "On Hysterical Anorexia."

35. L. Rahman, H. B. Richardson, and H. S. Ripley, "Anorexia Nervosa with Psychiatric Observations," *Psychom. Med.* 1 (1939): 335.

36. Binswanger, pp. 250–51, 244.

37. Ibid., pp. 262, 258.

38. Thoma, p. 253.

39. Ibid., pp. 67–70.

40. Bruch, *Eating Disorders*; also H. Bruch, "Anorexia Nervosa and Its Differential Diagnosis," p. 555; and H. Bruch, "Perceptual and Conceptual Disturbances in Anorexia Nervosa," *Psychosom. Med.* 24 (1962): 187.

41. Hillman, *Dream and the Underworld*, p. 170.

42. Ibid., p. 171; also Joanne Stroud, in her article "Flesh Gone in Inquiring of the Bone," *Dragonflies: Studies in Imaginal Psychology* 2/1 (1980): 23, notes the connection between Persephone and the anorexic; this also is discussed in C. Robinson, "Anorexia Nervosa—an Underworld Trip," presented to the International Congress of Analytical Psychologists in San Francisco, September 1980.

43. Gull (1874). Modern treatments include: inpatient regimes based on behavior modification; drugs (chlorpromazine and anti-depressants); electroshock therapy; psychotherapy; pre-frontal leucotomy. See Dally and Gomez, and Russell for thorough descriptions of these treatments.

44. See Hillman, *Dream and the Underworld*, pp. 66–67, for a discussion of this.

Chapter II: Female of Borders

1. Bruch, "Perceptual and Conceptual Disturbances in Anorexia Nervosa"; Selvini, *Self-Starvation*, p. 28; Dally and Gomez, *Anorexia Nervosa*, particularly the section "Body Image and Mirror Gazing" in chapter 3; Bruch, *Eating Disorders*, pp. 88 ff.; Bruch, *Golden Cage*, p. 77. In this last work one patient discusses this question of fat: "When I say I overeat, it may not be what you think. I feel I'm gorging myself when I eat more than one cracker with peanut butter" (p. 3). Also, Binswanger ("The Case of Ellen West") notes Ellen West's feelings: "I feel myself getting fatter, I tremble with dread of this, I am living in a state of panic. . . . As soon as I feel a pressure on my waist— I mean a pressure of my waistband—my spirit sinks, and I get a depression as severe as though it were a question of goodness knows what tragic affairs" (p. 251).

2. Hillman, *Dream and the Underworld*, pp. 28 f.

3. Dally and Gòmez, p. 47.

4. Ibid. Also, Bruch, *Golden Cage*, p. 94; Selvini, pp. 20 f.; Ushakov, "Anorexia Nervosa"; and Thoma, *Anorexia Nervosa*, p. 309.

5. Meyer and Weinroth, "Observations on Psychological Aspects of Anorexia Nervosa," p. 397.

6. Bruch, *Eating Disorders*, p. 98; *Golden Cage*, p. 25.

7. Binswanger, pp. 239, 261, 333.

8. Theander, "Anorexia Nervosa. A Psychiatric Investigation of 94 Patients."

9. Thoma, pp. 68, 72 ff.

10. Ibid., p. 76.

11. Ibid., p. 86; see also pp. 252–53. Also see Lorand, "Anorexia Nervosa: Report of a Case," p. 290, whose patient wants "to be an 'it,' neither man nor woman, but a sexless child."

12. Selvini has a clear discussion of this transition, pp. 7 f.; Bruch, *Eating Disorders*, p. 214.

13. Russell, "Anorexia Nervosa: Its Identity as an Illness and Its Treatment"; see particularly pp. 140, 142.

14. Rahman et al., "Anorexia Nervosa with Psychiatric Observations," pp. 357 ff. Also J. R. Blitzer, N. Rollins, and A. Blackwell, "Children Who Starve Themselves: Anorexia Nervosa," *Psychosom. Med.* 23 (1961): 369, who give evidence for the occurrence of amenorrhea before the development of anorexia.

15. On the relation of duplicity to an underworld perspective, see Hillman, *Dream and the Underworld*, p. 127.

16. Hillman, *Re-Visioning Psychology*, discusses the importance of enigma and duplicity for soul, pp. 152, 160. The themes of duplicity, threshold, crossroads, and borderlines all evoke Hecate and an underworld journey to understand what looks mysterious from an upperworld perspective: Jung and Kerényi, *Essays on a Science of Mythology*, pp. 112, 120.

17. G. Bachelard, *On Poetic Imagination and Reverie: Selections from the Works of Gaston Bachelard*, trans. Colette Gaudin (Indianapolis: Bobbs-Merrill, 1971), quoted in Hillman, *Dream and the Underworld*, p. 126, where he discusses Bachelard's contribution to a psychological understanding of duplicity.

18. See Dally and Gomez, p. 51, concerning modes of eating and the concoctions of the anorexic diet, which include radishes, raw parsnips, carrots, Dutch cabbage. Bruch, *Eating Disorders*, pp. 265–67, 271; Bruch, *Golden Cage*, pp. 3 f., 8. Binswanger also discusses Janet's case Nadia and her diet of two small portions of bouillon, one egg yolk, one teaspoon of vinegar, and one cup of very strong tea with lemon and her hostility to anyone who would disapprove (p. 331). Also, on eating in secret, see Robinson, "Anorexia Nervosa—An Underworld Trip," p. 3; Binswanger, pp. 245–46, 249.

19. Blitzer et al., pp. 373-75; also Bruch, *Eating Disorders*, p. 93. The psychoanalytic interpretation of anorexia, during the forties and fifties, was based on the anorexic's view that the food was alive and potentially dangerous. Based upon an analysis of two anorexic cases, Waller et al., "Anorexia Nervosa: A Psychosomatic Entity," describe the disorder symbolically, in terms of eating as symbolic impregnation. They see this conflict to be the core of all emotional disturbances of anorexia. Their interpretation is that the anorexic sees food as potent and her wish to be impregnated through the mouth results in compulsive eating. This then is followed by guilt and the rejection of food. They see this pregnancy fantasy connected to the anorexic's literal cessation of menstruation. Lorand, "Anorexia Nervosa: Report of a Case," agrees with this interpretation and offers clinical affirmation. He traces the eating disturbance to the poisonous connotation of food for the anorexic which pertains to oral impregnation fantasies, i.e., that the food could harm as much as pregnancy and sexual intercourse. In the anorexic's "deepest unconscious, her inability to eat expressed her wish to waste away and die" (p. 289). So there is a primary desire for impregnation, to get fat, have a big abdomen. This makes her guilt-ridden and results in the expression of the opposite: denial by vomiting to kill the "gross" in her. Meyer and Weinroth also confirm the Waller hypothesis of the unconscious symbolic value of eating as impregnation.

20. The differentiation of "anorexia" and "bulimia" has to do with the degree of literalization in which this cycle is performed. The anorexic (who apparently starves without extreme binging or vomiting) still undergoes an eat-purge cycle but usually is of the personality disposition which cannot tolerate the abundance and mess of the literal binge-vomit ritual. For her, five crackers instead of one and a half becomes a binge, and the purgation will most likely consist of a rigorous athletic or dance program. The bulimic is a woman who is caught within the entire anorexic syndrome but who has personality aspects allowing her to enact the eat-purge cycle more literally and sensually. She gorges huge quantities such as a gallon of ice cream and boxes of cookies and vomits many times daily. Unlike the obese woman, both the ascetic anorexic and the bulimic see themselves as fat though they are not and have a tyrannical drive to destruct through harmful purgation practices (extreme starving, exer-

cising, vomiting). Both essentially undergo the eat–purge cycle yet literalize this to various degrees depending, I think, on basic personality differences pertaining to the tolerance of earthy mass/mess. I am grateful to Jeanne Walker for pointing out to me the necessity for elucidating this distinction.

After further reflection, and put in more psychodynamic terms: the bond between the anorexic and bulimic is that both are in relation to a particularly tyrannical sort of mother's "animus" (cf. chapter 3 on, this volume). The difference is that the anorexic relates to this "animus" more through carrying the mother's "superego," the bulimic more through carrying the mother's "id."

21. Bruch, *Golden Cage*, pp. 83–87; Bruch, *Eating Disorders*, pp. 267–68; Selvini, p. 20.

22. Lasegue, "On Hysterical Anorexia," in Kaufman and Heiman.

23. J. H. Lloyd, "Hysterical Tremor and Hysterical Anorexia of a Severe Type," *Amer. J. Med. Sc.* 106 (1893): 264, 275.

24. Ibid., p. 277.

25. Meyer and Weinroth, p. 395.

26. Ibid., p. 393.

27. Bruch, *Golden Cage*, pp. 14–17, 73–74.

28. Bruch, *Golden Cage*, pp. 11–12.

29. Binswanger, pp. 239, 241, 242, 278, 282, 296.

30. J. A. Macculloch, "Fasting (Introductory and non-Christian)" in *Encyclopedia of Religion and Ethics*, ed. J. Hastings, vol. 5 (New York: Scribner, 1912), p. 758. Macculloch discusses the widespread practice of the Melanesians and Polynesians for the mother to abstain from certain foods before and after the birth of a child, as well as during menstruation. Using the examples of the Tlingits and Egyptians, Macculloch also describes fasting as an act of mourning, as well as a purificatory act and rite of preparation for the reception of inhuman presences. Also see C. Kerényi, *Eleusis: Archetypal Image of Mother and Daughter* (New York: Pantheon, 1967), pp. 13–94, for a discussion of the Eleusinian mysteries and purifications and fasting rites of the mystai (initiates) in preparation for the "vision," "the state of having seen" (in the sense of transformation, not perception) the divine presence, Kore (Persephone), Queen of the Dead.

31. Also, this fasting for Demeter relates to association of gender with this pathology (note 22, chapter 1, this volume). The issue here is that, even for the males who participate in it, anorexia nervosa is a

form for encountering the goddess. Jung and Kerényi, p. 138, note the historical evidence that the male initiate in the Eleusinian mysteries regarded himself as a goddess and not a god.

32. Kerényi, *Eleusis*, pp. 60–90. Also see his discussion on the relation of fasting to "vision," pp. 179–80.

33. Ibid., pp. 91–102. Also see Jung and Kerényi, p. 117: "The grain figure is essentially the figure of both origin and end, of mother and daughter; and just because of that it points beyond the individual to the universal and eternal."

34. L. R. Farnell, *The Cults of the Greek States*, 5 vols. (New Rochelle, New York: Caratzas, 1977), 2: 515. Also Hillman, *Dream and the Underworld*, pp. 39–40.

35. Binswanger, p. 254.

36. P. Berry discusses how shame reflects the connection of matter to psyche in "What's the Matter with Mother," Lecture No. 190 (London: Guild of Pastoral Psychology, 1978), pp. 7–8; reprinted in P. Berry, *Echo's Subtle Body* (Dallas: Spring Publications, Inc., 1982). Also, on the repulsion, Ellen West describes: "The thought of pancakes is still for me the most horrible thought there is." Binswanger continues, "Moreover, meat and fat, she says, are so repugnant that the mere thought of them nauseates her" (p. 251).

37. Dally and Gomez, pp. 48–49. Binswanger describes this obsession of Ellen West: "At the same time she becomes intensely preoccupied with calorie charts, recipes, etc. In every free minute she writes recipes of delectable dishes, puddings, desserts, etc., in her cookbook. She demands of those around her that they eat much and well, while she denies herself everything" (p. 249). See also Blitzer et al. on the anorexic's cooking, fascination with food and feeding others: "One would see a severely emaciated child pushing a loaded food cart down the hospital corridor, serving the other patients, and urging them to finish their meals" (p. 373).

Bruch, *Golden Cage*, pp. 75–76, describes the anorexic's intensified cooking: how in one home "the father avoided a conflict between the cook and his anorexic daughter by building a special kitchen for the daughter." Bruch, *Eating Disorders*, pp. 264, 267: Fern (no. 22), fourteen-years-old, would bake and cook immediately when she returned from school and refused to go to bed until her parents had eaten every morsel of the rich desserts. Dora (no. 26) made her brother get quite obese, since she was obsessed with the thought he was starving and would continually carry candy for him. Also, see Joyce Stroud, "Anorexia Nervosa and the Puer Archetype," *Lapis* 6 (1980): 45–46.

38. Dally and Gomez, p. 46, on the fact that a "tiny slice of toast readily becomes magnified into half a loaf."

39. Bruch, *Eating Disorders*, p. 93.

40. Dally and Gomez give a very thorough description of this in chapter 3.

41. Hillman's discussion of "Narcissus and the Dream," in *Dream and the Underworld*, pp. 119–23, nicely relates to this sense of reflection. In E. Gottheil, C. E. Backup, F. S. Cornelison, "Denial and Self-Image Confrontation in a Case of Anorexia Nervosa," *J. Nerv. Ment. Dis.* 148 (1969): 238, the authors note how the mirror reflects subtle body, while the film reflects literal body.

42. Particularly Bruch, *Eating Disorders* (pp. 334–76), and *Golden Cage* (pp. 62–63, 121–50) and Selvini (pp. 151–58) discuss and practice this sort of psychotherapy.

43. Macculloch, p. 762. He cites Apuleius's description of the thrice-repeated ten day abstinence from certain foods as well as the abstinence from wine and animal flesh before being initiated into the mysteries of Isis. Also, he describes the procedure of the Musquakie Indians in which the male initiate, after nine years of training, is sent on a nine-day fast in which he wanders through the woods and learns, from his dreams, what his "medicine" is to be. Macculloch then discusses fasting as a preparation for sacred or magical rituals in which, in the tribes of New Guinea, for example, the sorcerers and ancients fast in order to learn from their vivid dreams.

44. Bruch, *Golden Cage*, pp. 11–12, 60, 50–51.

45. Ibid., pp. 40, 48.

46. Gull, "Anorexia Nervosa" (1888), p. 517.

47. Crisp, "Clinical and Therapeutic Aspects of Anorexia Nervosa."

48. Bruch, *Eating Disorders*, pp. 218, 102–03, 278, 280, 376; Selvini, chapter 21.

49. This psychic multiplicity accounts for the multiple figures with whom the anorexic is identified in recent depth psychology papers: Joanne Stroud, "Flesh Gone in Inquiring of the Bone": *Puer, Persephone, Artemis*; Bani Shorter, "The Concealed Body Language of Anorexia Nervosa," paper presented to the International Congress

of Analytical Psychologists, San Francisco, September 1980: *Athene*; Marian Woodman, *The Owl Was a Baker's Daughter* (Toronto: Inner City Books, 1980): *Athene, Demeter, Dionysus*; Joyce Stroud: *Puer, Dionysus-Eros*; Christa Robinson: *Persephone, Dionysus*.

Also, it has been observed by the two following Jungian analysts that the psychic multiplicity of the anorexic relates to the way she can touch upon or carry the more "hidden" or inferior aspects of others. Woodman says: "It may be worth considering here that a highly intuitive, highly intelligent child, who has been raised in close intimacy with the parents, may be hypersensitive to all that is going on unconsciously in and out of the home. She may, in fact, be carrying the shadow in almost every situation she enters" (p. 80). Robinson also suggests: "They also tend to be generous generally speaking, they love to give material presents. The 'Euboulos' aspect is also expressed in the phenomenon that these daughters tend to be confidantes of the people around them, with an ability to contact strange and pathological persons without saying a word. We find a number of these girls in the intensive wards of hospitals, or in the dusty dry atmosphere of libraries—places where one only needs to 'be present' without relating to anyone" (p. 8).

50. Bruch, *Golden Cage*, pp. 45–46, 48, 70–71. Also see Thoma's description of Henrietta A.'s magical world (p. 76), which according to his interpretation results from her narcissistic attempt to escape reality and return to a safe childhood realm through regressive fantasy.

51. Bruch, "Conceptual Confusion in Eating Disorders," *J. Nerv. Ment. Dis.* 133 (1961): 46; Bruch, "Perceptual and Conceptual Disturbances in Anorexia Nervosa."

52. Hillman discusses the implications of this fallacy for psychology in Part IV of *Re-Visioning Psychology*: see particularly p. 197.

53. Hillman, *Dream and the Underworld*, p. 40.

54. Ushakov discusses how the anorexic as a child lacked the natural unsophistication of childhood and was extremely conscientious and respectable.

55. K. Kelley, G. E. Daniels, J. Poe, R. Easser and R. Monroe, "Psychological Correlations with Secondary Amenorrhea," *Psychom. Med.* 16 (1954): 129, 144. Also see: J. C. Nemiah, "Anorexia Nervosa," *Medicine* 29 (1950): 225.

56. Kelley et al., pp. 129–36, where they discuss the presence of strong erotic and ambivalent emotions, heightened sexual urges, and

a sense of a magical ability to destroy, all occurring during the menstrual period. Also, they describe (pp. 130–31) the significance of menstruation, since antiquity, in allowing the woman to receive supernatural presences and magical interferences. Macculloch ("Fasting") also discusses this.

57. Kelley et al., pp. 129–47.

58. These characteristics, as well as the anorexic's hyperactivities, antagonistic stance, and rigidities, distinguish anorexia from obesity. I think there is a difficulty in studying the obese figure, her imaginal landscape, and the voices accompanying her suffering and then making logical connections to the anorexic. An example of this attempt is Woodman, *The Owl Was a Baker's Daughter*, which actually is a study of obesity; only a small section is devoted (pp. 76–82) to anorexia. The experiments on which the study is based were done only with obese women. There is a danger of working within the image of an obese woman (and the imaginal realm accompanying that: Orphelia, owl/baker's daughter, Athena) and then stating that anorexia is within the same syndrome, with identical complexes, yet is merely the counterpart or reverse. She states, for example, "In this study, the Great Goddess either materializes in the obese or devours the anorexic" (p. 10) and "My study of obesity as a psychosomatic symptom in individual women led to the realization that obesity and anorexia nervosa are counterpoles of one neurosis" (p. 102). The two (obese woman and anorexic woman), however, offer us entirely different images of the female, each of which brings up a unique imaginal landscape with specific voices, emotions or lack of emotion, and different "possessions." Lumping them together or reversing them is a conceptual move we do to them; when left to themselves and allowed to inform us, they speak in different languages and become manifest through different images.

59. Perhaps her particular message allows us to understand researchers' observations on the prevalence of upper-class anorexics. Bruch based the title of her recent text, *The Golden Cage*, on this fact. The doctors assume that the disease is a rebellion against the material wealth and extravagance of the home, but perhaps the message is that the anorexic has found that wealth is invisible and immaterial too. Dally and Gomez report that seventy-seven percent of anorexics are from the top two social classes (chapter 4).

Chapter III: Tyrant of Fat

1. The etymological definition of "anorexia" is "absence of desire" (Selvini, *Self-Starvation*, p. 21). Selvini discusses the confusion which the title generated once it was found that anorexics continually desire food.

2. Some researchers have postulated that the unfulfilled hunger instinct *causes* bursts of compensatory activity in the imagination. See Thoma, *Anorexia Nervosa*, quoting Katz, p. 274, for a discussion of how hunger generates tensions which cause movement in the imagination; also his statement that obsessively feeding others shows how the anorexic uses imagination to satisfy hunger (p. 254).

3. Ibid., p. 18.

4. W. W. Gull, "Address on Medicine," *Lancet* 2 (1868): 171.

5. Meyer and Weinroth, "Psychological Aspects of Anorexia Nervosa," p. 393.

6. Bruch, *Golden Cage*, p. 55.

7. Bruch, personal communication, June 1980.

8. Bruch, *Golden Cage*, p. 10; also see pp. 62–63.

9. Binswanger, "The Case of Ellen West," p. 259.

10. Ibid., pp. 251, 258. Also, the patient described by Gottheil et al., "Denial and Self-Image Confrontation in a Case of Anorexia Nervosa," states: "There is something inside of me that I have to get out and I don't know what it is. I feel angry at myself." This "voice of her own mind" told her she didn't have the right to try to be like the healthy, pretty women she saw in advertisements (p. 242).

11. Binswanger, pp. 245, 285.

12. See Hillman, *Dream and the Underworld*, p. 45, for an elaboration of this figure. It is interesting to note here that in discussing Ellen West's understanding of death within life, Binswanger briefly refers to Heraclitus's fragment 51 on the interchangeability of Hades/Dionysus (p. 294 and n. 63). See also Kerényi, *Eleusis*, pp. 35, 40.

13. Woodman, *Owl Was a Baker's Daughter*, discusses how the obese woman also is possessed by a "demon" (pp. 54, 56, 57, 61, 70, 74). Yet note that this possession, which she discusses in terms of a "negative animus" (pp. 74, 75, 98), does not strike the obese woman in the same form as the anorexic's tyrannical antagonism and rigid compulsiveness; for the obese woman it relates more to the body's literal fatty layers and swellings.

14. Bruch, *Golden Cage*, p. 62. Also, Meyer and Weinroth give the example of a patient who, to test herself, would introduce a spoonful of ice cream into her mouth and withdraw it without tasting or touching it (p. 393).

15. Bruch, *Golden Cage*, pp. 16–17.

16. Binswanger, p. 255.

17. Selvini, chapters 3 and 4. Also, in Rahman et al., "Anorexia Nervosa with Psychiatric Observations," see particularly the first six cases diagnosed as psychoneurotic reactions with compulsive features. Ushakov, "Anorexia Nervosa," discusses how, even being quite asthenic and emaciated, the anorexic persists on any set task, reacts violently to opposition, and tackles physical work beyond her strength. Thoma says: "It is the anorexia nervosa patient's antagonistic attitude that has proved the chief stumbling block for every investigator since Gull and Lasegue" (p. 299).

18. Lasegue, quoted in Kaufman and Heiman, *Evolution*, p. 148.

19. Binswanger, p. 252, on the walking ritual; and see also Bruch, *Eating Disorders*, pp. 272–75, and *Golden Cage*, pp. 5–6, for specific examples of physical activity.

20. Thoma, p. 275; see also Binswanger, p. 291.

21. Bruch, *Eating Disorders*, p. 271; Dally and Gomez, *Anorexia Nervosa*, p. 66.

22. Thoma, p. 257; Bruch, *Golden Cage*, p. 88; Bruch, *Eating Disorders*, pp. 270–71, describes how the context for a binge is what the patients call "emptiness" in the sense of a lack of feeling or intimacy with another. It is this void, this ultimate dissolution, which drives the anorexic to gorge herself with food (or activity) as though that might fill the abysmal hole.

23. Thoma, p. 250.

24. Binswanger, p. 284.

25. Thoma describes this phenomenon which he refers to as a "cosmic surrender to the wind" (p. 277); also he says: "They seem to have no more needs, and every offer of help is experienced as a danger which could threaten the perfection and security which they have achieved through partial disavowal of reality. They appear unmoved by their own physical deterioration; this can be traced back to a delusional belief that they are capable of living on their own substance, in a kind of autarchy" (p. 249). We have been inquiring in-

stead on what substance they live, and this inquiry has taken us to psychic substance.

26. Bruch, *Eating Disorders*, p. 258.

27. Hillman, *Myth of Analysis*, pp. 263, 275.

Chapter IV: Mother of Skeletal Lady

1. Meyer and Weinroth, "Psychological Aspects of Anorexia Nervosa," p. 395.

2. J. C. Nemiah, "Anorexia Nervosa, Fact and Theory," *Amer. J. Dig. Dis.* 3 (1958): 249, quoted in V. Taipale, O. Tuomi, and M. Aukee, "Anorexia Nervosa. An Illness of Two Generations?", *Acta Paedopsychiat.* 38 (1971): 21.

3. Thoma, *Anorexia Nervosa*, p. 261.

4. A. King, "Primary and Secondary Anorexia Nervosa Syndromes," pp. 471, 472, 475, 476.

5. Theander, "A Psychiatric Investigation of 94 Female Patients," pp. 162-63, 159, 168-69.

6. Blitzer et al., "Children Who Starve Themselves: Anorexia Nervosa," p. 379; also O. Fenichel, "Anorexia," in *Collected Papers of O. Fenichel*, vol. 2 (London: Routledge and Kegan Paul, 1955). Using two brief cases, Fenichel discusses the relation of anorexia to the dominant mother and pre-genital fixation.

7. Bruch, *Golden Cage*, pp. 29-30. Also see A. Barcai, "Family Therapy in the Treatment of Anorexia Nervosa," *Amer. J. of Psychiat.* 128 (1971): 286.

8. Bruch, *Golden Cage*, pp. 67-69. Bruch discusses a mother's mastectomy as a precipitating factor of a daughter's illness (p. 68); Dally and Gomez, *Anorexia Nervosa*, also describe the mother's illness as a significant factor, with carcinoma as an example, chapter 4.

9. W. Otto, "The Meaning of the Eleusinian Mysteries," in *The Mysteries. Papers from the Eranos Yearbooks*, ed. Joseph Campbell, Bollingen Series (Princeton: Princeton University Press, 1978), p. 16. Also Kerényi, *Eleusis*, on the duality of Demeter-Persephone, pp. 32-33, 144-50. Jung and Kerényi, *Essays on a Science of Mythology*, state: "They are to be thought of as a *double figure*, one half of which is the ideal complement of the other. Persephone is, above all,

her *mother's* kore: without her, Demeter would not be a *Meter*" (p. 109); see also pp. 178–79.

10. "The Hymn to Demeter," in *The Homeric Hymns*, trans. Charles Boer (Spring Publications, 1979), pp. 90 ff. Also see W. Otto, "The Meaning of the Eleusinian Mysteries." For a psychological discussion of Demetrian consciousness, in terms of clinging to an upperworld perspective and denying underworld consciousness, see P. Berry, "The Rape of Demeter/Persephone and Neurosis," *Spring 1975*: 190 f.

11. Blitzer et al., particularly pp. 368–73.

12. Dally and Gomez, chapter 4. D. W. K. Kay, K. Shapira, and S. Brandon, "Some Early Factors of Anorexia Nervosa Compared to Non-Anorexic Groups," *J. Psychom. Res.* 11 (1967): 133.

13. Bruch discusses this background in all her work: see specifically "Hunger and Instinct," *J. Nerv. Ment. Dis.* 149 (1969): 91; and *Golden Cage*, pp. 26, 40–41. In a personal communication, she described the mother as "gifted and frustrated."

14. Taipale et al., p. 24.

15. Hillman's discussion of the numb and deadened heart, which falls into "evil" conventionalities and formalisms, is helpful here: "The Thought of the Heart," in *Eranos Jahrbuch 48—1979* (Frankfurt a/M: Insel Verlag, 1981), pp. 172–76.

16. See Jung and Kerényi on this: "Every grain of wheat and every maiden contains, as it were, all of its descendants and all her descendants—an infinite series of mothers and daughters in one" (p. 153); "We could therefore say that every mother contains her daughter in herself and every daughter her mother, and that every woman extends backwards into her mother and forwards into her daughter" (p. 162); "It is one thing to know about the 'seed and the sprout' and quite another to have *recognized* in them the past and future as one's own being and its continuation. Or, as Professor Jung puts it: to experience the return, the *apocatastasis*, of one's ancestors in such a way that these can prolong themselves via the bridge of the momentary individual into the generations of the future. A knowledge with this content, with the experience of *being in death*, is not to be despised" (pp. 181–82).

Chapter V: The Gaping Mouth

1. "The Hymn to Demeter," trans. C. Boer, pp. 92–97.
2. Bruch, *Golden Cage*, p. 60.
3. Blitzer et al., "Children Who Starve Themselves: Anorexia Nervosa," pp. 370–83.
4. M. Selvini, "The Families of Patients with Anorexia Nervosa," in *The Child in His Family*, ed. J. Anthony and C. Koupernik (New York: Wiley, 1970), pp. 323–27.
5. "The Hymn to Demeter," pp. 98–102.
6. This points back to the "original *identity* of mother and daughter," Jung and Kerényi, *Essays on a Science of Mythology*, p. 121. Mythologically, we find that Demeter is present in Persephone's realm as Persephone's experience also is in Demeter's: the swineherd's pigs (Demeter's sacrificial animal) were swallowed in the earth along with Persephone (p. 118); also, in one source of the myth, Demeter is raped by Poseidon as she is looking for her ravished daughter (p. 123).
7. Bruch discusses the literalization of the anorexic, *Golden Cage*, pp. 48, 62, 70.
8. C. Robinson also discusses the vomiting portion of the ritual in terms of a "dematerialization or Hades" and relates this to that quality of Hades connected with *Ais* or *Aides*, he-who-makes-invisible, "Anorexia Nervosa—An Underworld Trip," p. 7.
9. The anorexic "gobbling" mother's food in the kitchen evokes the tale of Demeter who, consumed by grief for her missing daughter, eats Pelops's shoulder without awareness of what it is she furiously is gobbling. P. Berry notes the tale ("Demeter/Persephone and Neurosis," n. 11), citing H. J. Rose, *A Handbook of Greek Mythology* (London: Methuen and Co., Ltd., 1965), p. 81. The "compulsive grasping" of the anorexic reminds us of Hillman's statement in *Re-Visioning Psychology*, p. 116, *"Sometimes we act in order not to see. I may well be actively doing and taking part in order to avoid knowing what my soul is doing and what interior person has a stake in the action"* (his italics).
10. Successful outcome for this disease is not promising. Selvini, *Self-Starvation*, chapter 22, cites her figures: out of eight anorexics seen in a clinic, only one could be said to have stabilized her weight with good social and sexual adaptation, yet she still was "frigid." Out

of twenty-two private patients, only twelve were "cured." Dally and Gomez summarize the larger surveys (Crisp, Theander, Thoma, and Bruch), stating that recovery is estimated at about fifty percent. Bemis, "Current Approaches to the Etiology and Treatment of Anorexia Nervosa," discusses (pp. 597–600) numerous studies which attempt to delineate factors indicating a differential prediction of outcome of anorexia nervosa. Bemis states that despite a favorable initial response to treatment, follow-up reports indicate that fewer than one half of anorexic patients "achieve a satisfactory adjustment" (p. 597) with symptoms reoccurring for twenty-five to fifty percent of patients, and thirty-eight percent requiring readmission for anorexia nervosa within two years.

11.   Gottheil et al., "Denial and Self-Image Confrontation in a Case of Anorexia Nervosa," p. 238.

12.   Ibid., p. 248.

13.   Ibid., p. 242.

14.   We have to be grateful for Dr. Bruch's contributions here: the abundance of research and thought she has put into this topic over decades. Her rich phenomenological observations and ability to steer away from systematic interpretation have offered us much insight into the nature and form of this pathology. Therefore, the following criticism is offered only in the spirit of advancing her observations further.

15.   Bruch, *Golden Cage*, pp. 15, 13, 21, 87; see also 16–17, 40–44.

16.   Ibid., pp. 101–03.

17.   Ibid., p. 111.

18.   Ibid., p. 135. Note the extreme difference between this and Hillman's perspective that it is within the inferiority, the incompetence, that one finds the deepest psychic figures, as well as his approach of "actively being engaged in imagining, and particularly with inferior imagining: images of inferiors and images that make us behave inferiorly" (J. Hillman, "Psychotherapy's Inferiority Complex," in *Eranos Jahrbuch 46—1977* [Frankfurt a/M: Insel Verlag, 1981], p. 8; revised in *Healing Fiction* [Barrytown, New York: Station Hill Press, 1983]).

19.   Bruch, *Golden Cage*, p. 145.

20.   Ibid., p. 142.

21.   Bruch, "Hunger and Instinct," p. 94; *Eating Disorders*, p. 337; *Golden Cage*, p. 123.

22. Selvini, *Self-Starvation*, pp. 193–230. Also, Barcai, "Family Therapy in the Treatment of Anorexia Nervosa," pp. 286–90.

Chapter VI: Gaia's Sickle

1. Which makes it all the more surprising that anorexia has never been a favored child of depth psychology. Freud only made occasional references to anorexia nervosa. In *The Origins of Psycho-Analysis: Letters to Wilhelm Fliess, Drafts and Notes, 1887–1902*, ed. Marie Bonaparte et al. and trans. Eric Mosbacher and James Strachey (New York: Basic Books, 1954), Freud writes, "The nutritional neurosis parallel to melancholia is anorexia. The well-known *anorexia nervosa* (F's italics) of girls seems to me (on careful observation) to be a melancholia occurring where sexuality is undeveloped. The patient asserts that she has not eaten simply because she has no appetite and for no other reason. Loss of appetite—in sexual terms, loss of libido" (p. 103). And in *On Psychotherapy* (*SE*, 7: 257–68), he writes, in 1905, "Psychoanalysis should not be attempted when the speedy removal of dangerous symptoms is required as, for example, in a case of hysterical anorexia" (p. 264). Hillman notes the neglect of food and eating in the works of depth psychologists in *Dream and the Underworld*, p. 173.

2. Berry, "What's the Matter with Mother," pp. 5, 9, 16–19; and also "Demeter/Persephone and Neurosis."

3. D. H. Lawrence's letter to Lady Ottoline Morell (March 1915): "Do you know Cassandra in Aeschylus and Homer? She is one of the world's great figures, and what the Greeks and Agamemnon did to her is symbolic of what mankind has done to her since—raped and despoiled and mocked her, to their own ruin. It is not your brain you must trust to, nor your will—but to that fundamental pathetic faculty for receiving the hidden waves that come from the depths of life, and for transferring them to the unreceptive world. It is something which happens below the consciousness, and below the range of the will—it is something which is unrecognized and frustrated and destroyed" (*Collected Letters*, ed. Harry T. Moore, vol. 1 [New York: The Viking Press, 1962], p. 326; quoted in Aeschylus, *The Oresteia*, trans. R. Fagles [New York: The Viking Press, 1975], p. 331, n. 1196).

4. See Hillman, *Dream and the Underworld*, on this: the "gap" is what accompanies and necessitates Hades. Hillman states: "Hades is

said to have had no temples or altars in the upperworld and his confrontation with it is experienced as a violence, a violation (Persephone's rape, the assaults on simple vegetative nymphs, Leuce and Minthe; and *Iliad*, 5, 395 and Pindar 01.9, 33)" (pp. 27–28).

5. J. H. Masserman, "Psychodynamics in Anorexia Nervosa and Neurotic Vomiting." Masserman takes the interpretation by Waller et al. (eating as oral impregnation) a step further.

6. Selvini, "The Families of Patients of Anorexia Nervosa," p. 327; Thoma, *Anorexia Nervosa*, p. 261.

7. *On Poetic Imagination and Reverie: Selections from the Works of Gaston Bachelard*, trans. Colette Gaudin, pp. 14 ff., quoted in Hillman, "Silver and the White Earth (Part Two)," *Spring 1981*: 60.

8. Otto, "The Meaning of the Eleusinian Mysteries," pp. 24–30.

9. Hesiod, *Theogony*, trans. Richard Lattimore (Ann Arbor: University of Michigan Press, 1973), pp. 132–34.

10. Ibid., pp. 134 f.

11. C. Kerényi, *The Gods of the Greeks* (London: Thames and Hudson, 1979), pp. 22–23; also on Kronos's fixedness, J. Hillman, "On Senex Consciousness," *Spring 1970*; and "On Senex Destruction and a Renaissance Solution," *Spring 1975*.

12. T. Burckhardt, *Alchemy* (Baltimore: Penguin, 1974), p. 187; also see pp. 185–87 where he discusses the first stage of the work corresponding to "blackening" and "mortification," and which comes under the sign of Saturn/Kronos. Getting caught in Kronos could keep the starving woman stuck within the first stage of her psychological journey. She could enact Kronos's repetitious absorption of matter if she forgets the sickle. Also see Hillman on Senex, *Spring 1970, 1975*.

13. C. G. Jung on this psychological inheritance: "I feel very strongly that I am under the influence of things or questions which were left incomplete and unanswered by my parents and grandparents and more distant ancestors. It often seems as if there were an impersonal karma within a family, which is passed on from parents to children. It has always seemed to me that I had to answer questions which fate had posed to my forefathers, and which had not yet been answered, or as if I had to complete, or perhaps continue, things which previous ages had left unfinished" (*Memories, Dreams, Reflections* [New York: Random House, 1965], p. 233).

14. The alchemical process which corresponds with this situation is vitrification: see Hillman, "Silver and the White Earth (Part Two)," pp. 38–39. If a redness continues in the nigredo (black) stage, this vitrification results in a hardening as well as an acting-out, compulsivity, emotionality (reddening).

Chapter VII: Imaginal Therapy

1. For a thorough study of "daimon" and its relation to psychotherapy based on Jung's work, see J. Hillman, "The Pandaemonium of Images: C. G. Jung's Contribution to *Know Thyself*," *New Lugano Review* 3 (1977): 35–45; and for a summary of references relating to daimon, see n. 2, chapter VIII, this volume.

2. Jung and Kerényi, *Essays on a Science of Mythology*, p. 127, on the connection of the sickle—"moon-shaped instrument [which] has been used for the cutting of that which *bears the seed*, i.e., the standing corn" (their italics)—with Demeter/Persephone.

3. Burckhardt, *Alchemy*, p. 186: see his discussion of the first (nigredo) stage of the work, corresponding to "blackening" and "mortification." He continues to state that Christian mysticism speaks of this state in terms of "the parable of the grain of wheat, which must remain alone in the earth and die, if it is to bring forth fruit" (p. 186).

4. "The Hymn to Demeter," trans. C. Boer, pp. 102–07.

5. The Homeric hymn calls the jesting daughter Iambe; Paul Friedrich discusses the possibility of the importance of iambic verse in the Eleusinian Mysteries and notes also that Iambe's quipping may be related to the obscene verbal behavior "common in fertility rites in general, [which] is thought to stimulate the productive powers of the earth" (*The Meaning of Aphrodite* [Chicago: University of Chicago Press, 1978], p. 172). Nor Hall states that, according to an Orphic version of the myth, Iambe is called Baubo who brought forth Demeter's smile through suggestive dances, obscene spread-legged gestures, and "belly laughs" (*The Moon and the Virgin*). "Baubo" figurines are known from Ptolemaic Egypt (second through third centuries) and are described as fat, seated, and displaying the genitalia. "The figurines, sometimes as small as amulets, appear to have been found near or within the women's rooms in Egyptian houses, and they appear to have been connected with a so-called Bubastis cult, exclusive

to women and connected with childbirth and the promotion of fertility" (Jorgen Andersen, *The Witch on the Wall* [Copenhagen: Rosenkilde and Bagger, 1977], pp. 133–34). The connection to female fertility cults evokes the rites of the witches of the fourteenth through the seventeenth centuries. Indeed, Andersen notes that Frau Baubo rides a sow followed by witches in the Walpurgisnacht festivities in Goethe's *Faust* (p. 19, n. 42). The entire anorexia syndrome can be likened to the phenomena of the witch (on a psychological reading of the witch, see my "Verso una comprensione psicologica della strega," *Giornale storico di psicologia dinamica* 7 [1983]: 44), yet that discussion lies outside the scope of this study.

    6. "The Hymn to Demeter," p. 107.

    7. Ibid.

    8. Ibid., pp. 108–13.

    9. Hillman, "Pandaemonium of Images," p. 42.

    10. "The Hymn to Demeter," pp. 113–20.

    11. Ibid., pp. 120–23.

    12. Ibid., pp. 123–35.

    13. For my image of Hecate, I have drawn from the works of: Hesiod, *Theogony*, pp. 147–49; C. Kerényi, *Gods of the Greeks*, pp. 35 f., 113, 233, 140; Farnell, *The Cults of the Greek States*, vol. 2, pp. 501–19; R. Graves, *The Greek Myths: 1* (Baltimore: Penguin, 1966), pp. 122–24; C. Kerényi, *Hermes, Guide of Souls* (Spring Publications, 1976), p. 65. Also see my paper on the witch, "Verso una comprensione psicologica della strega." Lectures by and conversations with David Miller have contributed to my understanding of Hecate. I am very grateful for the support and encouragement he offered me at the early stages of the writing of this manuscript.

    14. On thymos (breath-soul/blood-soul) and its connection with lungs, lung disease, and love disease for the Homeric and Pre-Socratic Greeks, see R. B. Onians, *The Origins of European Thought* (Cambridge: Cambridge University Press, 1951), particularly pp. 37, 56 f. Other discussions of thymos and breathing are found in R. J. Sardello, "Beauty and Violence," *Dragonflies: Studies in Imaginal Psychology* 2/1 (1980): 93 f.; T. Moore, "Images in Asthma," *Dragonflies* 1/2 (1979): 10; M. Sipiora, "A Soul's Journey," *Spring 1981*: 165–67.

    15. Nursing through breath is psychological nursing: the sisters of baby Demophoön became "inferior nurses" after the nursing of Demeter. Demeter's nursing served as an initiation to the fire of the

underworld, to the realm of inhuman essence, to soul; she was a psychological nurse.

16. This relates to Hillman's warning about conversion, in discussing the psychological transition from the black, inert, materialized, nigredo stage to the white awakening of psychic reality in the albedo stage: the albedo must always be distinguished from the prima materia. "Here the whitening converts back to primary innocence and the opus is back where it began" ("Silver and the White Earth [Part Two]," p. 35).

17. Mary Watkins states this well in "Six Approaches to the Image in Art Therapy," *Spring 1981*: 117: "The image in its specificity lends us the imaginal background to each experience, thus raising the day-world onto the plane of metaphorical meanings. As image and experience interpenetrate, the image is not discarded but becomes an eye through which one perceives and senses."

18. On the spontaneous images arising in a method called "active imagination," Jung writes that it is "a method (devised by myself) of introspection for observing the stream of interior images. One concentrates one's attention on some impressive but unintelligible dream-image, or on a spontaneous visual impression, and observes the changes taking place in it. . . . The advantage of this method is that it brings a mass of unconscious material to light. Drawing, painting, and modelling can be used to the same end. Once a visual series has become dramatic, it can easily pass over into the auditive or linguistic sphere and give rise to dialogues and the like" (Jung and Kerényi, p. 164). For Jung's discussion of his own work with active imagination, see his *Memories, Dreams, Reflections.* See also Hillman on this: "Jung says he treated the figures whom he met 'as though they were real people'. The key is that *as though*; the metaphorical, 'as-if' reality, neither literally real (hallucinations or people in the street) nor ir-real/unreal (mere fictions, projections which 'I' make up as parts of 'me', optical illusions)" ("Pandaemonium of Images," p. 36). He continues to contrast active imagination with introspection (p. 36), to conventional morality (p. 37), and demonology (pp. 38–42), and presents six cautions about it concerning spirituality, artistic production, mystical vision, and personal cure (pp. 42–43). Also, on the tradition of speaking directly with the soul, with examples from his practice, see Hillman, "Psychotherapy's Inferiority Complex." See also Mary Watkins's discussion of Jung's personal and professional work with

active imagination, *Waking Dreams* (New York: Harper & Row, 1976), pp. 42–51, as well as her excellent account of therapeutic "imagining," chapters 6, 7, 8.

19. Hillman, "Silver and the White Earth (Part Two)," p. 47.

20. Ibid.

21. That is, active engagement through active imagination and dialoguing with the figures. See Hillman, "Psychotherapy's Inferiority Complex," for examples of this.

22. J. Hillman, "Silver and the White Earth (Part One)," *Spring 1980*: 23.

23. Hillman discusses the importance of this for psychological awakening, *Re-Visioning Psychology*, pp. 14–15.

Chapter VIII: Daimon Ice Woman w/ Bitch

1. See Binswanger, "The Case of Ellen West," for descriptions of Ellen's poetry; also in relation to this, see the poem by June Jordan, quoted in Kim Chernin, *The Obsession*, p. 12. I would like to add that it would have been difficult, if not impossible, for me to write the latter sections of this book without the "space" in Connecticut provided by my colleagues Michele Toomey and Helen Yott.

2. On Daimones: "the *daimones* were figures of the middle realm, neither quite transcendent Gods nor quite physical humans, and there were many sorts of them, beneficial, terrifying, message-bringers, mediators, voices of guidance and caution (as Socrates' Daimon and as Diotima)" (Hillman, "Pandaemonium of Images," p. 36). Also see this paper for a discussion of Jung's daimones: "personified images of interior vision. . . . This encounter with these personal figures became the first personifications of his mature *fate*—which is also how Jung speaks of the personifications we meet when we interiorize to Know Thyself" (pp. 35 f.). See also Jung, *Memories, Dreams, Reflections*; and vol. 7 and vol. 17, pp. 175 ff. of *The Collected Works of C. G. Jung* (hereinafter *CW*), Bollingen Series XX (Princeton: Princeton University Press and London: Routledge and Kegan Paul, 1953–79). For other studies of daimon, see Onians, *The Origins of European Thought*; E. R. Dodds, "Man and the Daemonic World," in *Pagan and Christian in an Age of Anxiety* (Cambridge: Cambridge University Press, 1965); R. May, "Psychotherapy

and the Daimonic," in *Myths, Dreams, and Religion*, ed. J. Campbell (New York: Dutton, 1970), pp. 196–210. On Socrates' daimon, see Plato, *Phaedrus*, 242c; *Apology*, 91d; and on Plato's discussion of it, see P. Friedlander, "Demon and Eros," chapter 2 in *Plato*, vol. 1, Bollingen Series (Princeton: Princeton University Press, 1973). Also, Ficino on daimon guardians in *Marsilio Ficino: The Book of Life*, trans. C. Boer (Spring Publications, 1980), pp. 169–73. Not much has been written on the woman's relation to daimon, except there is some discussion of this in one fascinating piece by Adrienne Rich: "Vesuvius at Home: The Power of Emily Dickinson," in *On Lies, Secrets, and Silence* (New York: W. W. Norton, 1979).

3. Binswanger quotes Ellen West on this: "'The sight of the groceries awakens longings in me which they [the groceries] can never still. As though a person tried to quench his thirst with ink. Perhaps I would find liberation if I could solve this puzzle: The connection between eating and longing'" (p. 254).

4. In the sense of Know Thyself: "Know Thyself in Jung's manner means to become familiar with, to open oneself to and listen to, that is, to know and discern, daimons" (Hillman, "Pandaemonium of Images," p. 35).

5. Thoma, *Anorexia Nervosa*, p. 37, comments that the only aspect of the treatment agreed upon unanimously is that patients must be removed from the home environment.

6. For my discussion of sulfur, I have used the following references: Jung, *CW* 14, §134–53, *CW* 12; Burckhardt, *Alchemy*; Hillman, "The Thought of the Heart," where he draws from the works of John Read, *Through Alchemy to Chemistry* (London: Bell, 1957), p. 18; "New Chemical Light" in *Hermetic Museum*, vol. 2 (London: Stuart and Watkins, 1953), p. 154; and from Paracelsus, *The Hermetic and Alchemical Writings*, trans. A. E. Waite, vol. 1 (New York: University Books, 1967), p. 127.

Also, I have drawn directly from chemistry sources: J. R. Partington, *A Textbook of Inorganic Chemistry* (New York: Macmillan and Co., 1950), pp. 447–51; James Norris, *A Textbook of Inorganic Chemistry for Colleges* (New York: McGraw-Hill, 1921), pp. 245–47; M. J. Sienko and R. A. Plane, *Chemistry* (New York: McGraw-Hill, 1966).

Thanks go to Bonnie Rosenberg for her assistance in obtaining these references.

7. Norris, *Inorganic Chemistry for Colleges*, p. 245. In this relation to fire and brimstone, and also because of sulfur's connection to volcanoes, its abundance in Sicily, and relation to skin irritation and rash, the metaphorical association is made between sulfur and the color red.

8. Dylan Thomas, *Collected Poems: 1934-1952* (London: Everyman's Library, 1977), p. 8. Also see Burckhardt, p. 140, on the connection of sulfur with the sun, the lion, the vitality of the world.

9. See Jung, *CW* 14, §151-52 for the connection of sulfur to "compulsion."

10. Related to this view, Chernin states: "What might be seen as great and heroic in us, worthy of respect and admiration, is lost because we have as yet no universal language to discuss a woman's struggle for the soul" (*Obsession*, p. 187). Also, Hélène Cixous, "Castration or Decapitation?", *Signs* 7 (1981): 41: "The unconscious is always cultural and when it talks it tells you your old stories, it tells you the old stories you've heard before because it consists of the repressed of culture. But it's also always shaped by the forceful return of a libido that doesn't give up that easily, and also by what is strange, what is outside culture, by a language which is a savage tongue that can make itself understood quite well. This is why, I think, *political* and not just literary work is started as soon as writing gets done by women that goes beyond the bounds of censorship, reading, the gaze, the masculine command, in that cheeky risk taking women can get into when they set out into the unknown to look for themselves" (pp. 52-53).

11. Norris, p. 246. Also "New Chemical Light" in *Hermetic Museum*, vol 2, p. 154, quoted in Hillman, "The Thought of the Heart," p. 140.

12. "Sulfur can be got from whatever catches our attention, blazes up. It comes from the natural world and our worldliness. It may be mined from any compulsion, fascination or attraction in the macrocosm" (Hillman, "Silver and the White Earth [Part One]," p. 32). Also see Hillman's discussion of this in "The Thought of the Heart," p. 141, pp. 176-82; also Jung, *CW* 14, §151-52.

13. This containment and refinement of red sulfur, so that its desire vitalizes and releases the soul without consumption, metaphorically signifies a move from red sulfur to white sulfur: Hillman, "Silver and the White Earth (Part One)," pp. 28-30; "Part Two,"

pp. 40–44; also "The Thought of the Heart." Hillman compares white sulfur with silver, discussing their "innate affinity" ("Silver and the White Earth [Part One]," pp. 28–30), and in continuing to discuss silver-mining in medieval and renaissance alchemy, he notes the connection of cold/hate with white sulfur (pp. 38–39) and also 'sound' as a place of silver-mining (pp. 41–46).

14. Kerényi, *Gods of the Greeks*, p. 58.

15. For an insightful discussion of this, see Friedrich, *The Meaning of Aphrodite*, chapter 5.

16. See Chapter VI, this volume, n. 3.

17. Kerényi, *Gods of the Greeks*, p. 34.

18. Dante, "Canto IX," lines 38–42 in *The Divine Comedy: Hell*, trans. Dorothy L. Sayers (New York: Penguin, 1980), p. 124.

19. Kerényi, *Gods of the Greeks*, p. 47.

20. Ibid., p. 49. Also see Jung and Kerényi, *Essays on a Science of Mythology*, pp. 125–26, on the terrible aspects of Persephone.

21. Image from the song "Native Dancer," written by Cris Williamson and on her album *Strange Paradise*, Olivia Records, Inc., 1980. Also the music of Kay Gardner greatly contributed in the writing of this chapter, as did the heartfelt spirit of Bloodroot of Connecticut. I am grateful also for Bloodroot's reading of and feedback on the "mother sections" at the early stages of the writing of this manuscript.

22. One attribute of sulfur—"fatness of the earth"—in *Libellus de Alchimia*, ascribed to Albertus Magnus, quoted in Hillman, "The Thought of the Heart," p. 140. Also, sulfur occurs in many oils found in plants, such as onions, mustard, garlic, cabbage (Norris, p. 246).

23. Including the father. Since the anorexic is struggling with a Hades tyrannical force connected to Mother, mother's choice of husband may also carry this Hades element which would account for some of the dramatic images of father's rapaciousness alongside descriptions of his awesomeness and majesty, in Bani Shorter, "The Concealed Body Language of Anorexia Nervosa," pp. 11–12.

24. This connects us to the *non-being* of Persephone, which is "not *pure* non-being, rather the sort of non-being from which the living shrink as from something *with a negative sign*: a monstrosity that has usurped the place of the unimaginably beautiful, the nocturnal aspect of what by day is the most desirable of all things" (Jung and Kerényi, pp. 127–28 [their italics]).

25. The danger of "conversion" in the transition to psychic reality of which Hillman speaks in "Silver and the White Earth (Part Two)," pp. 34–35.

26. In the sense of "being consumed" by the desire. On Hecate's bite, allowing the distance needed to see through instead of literalizing or compulsively acting out, we recall that the most common etymology for her name comes from hekatos, "the distant one" (Kerényi, *Gods of the Greeks*, p. 35). Also, we see that such work with imaginal presences allows us to find a "differentiated ego" which knows its own boundaries by going *to* soul and by way of the figures in soul instead of "constructing ego" (with a focus on personal intention, feeling, and behavior) at the expense of intrapsychic reality.

27. See Sappho on the association of Hecate with Aphrodite (Fragment 35): "You wear her livery / Shining with gold, / you, too, Hecate, / Queen of Night, hand- / maid to Aphrodite" (*Sappho*, trans. Mary Barnard [Berkeley and Los Angeles: University of California Press, 1958]).

28. Hecate's light is not as direct as the sun's: "She is in her cave when the sun sees the seduction" (Jung and Kerényi, p. 110); and see pp. 110–11 on Hecate's torch. This is the light needed to soften the glare which so transfixes and tyrannizes the anorexic (so red sulfur can become white sulfur).

29. See Otto, "The Meaning of the Eleusinian Mysteries," p. 30.

30. Hillman, "The Thought of the Heart," p. 161, n. 37.

31. Binswanger, p. 252.

32. I disagree with Kerényi here that Persephone is "completely passive" (in her picking the stupefying flowers when she was raped), *Essays on a Science of Mythology*, p. 108. The paradox is that *within* the active grasp is the stupefaction (the blindness and numbness of the compulsion).

33. Onians, pp. 74–75. Also, working from that book, J. Hillman ("The Thought of the Heart," pp. 163–65) discusses "taking in," "breathing in," and "gasp" as *aisthesis*, the activity of aesthetic perception and the link between heart and senses. Recall Helen's breathing problem, which suggests an inability to take in, draw from, the figurations of the heart, the imaginal presences. With an education of active imagination and dream work, she began to "take in," "breathe in" the world in the sense of aesthetic reaction. Also, see Hillman's discussion in that paper of Aphrodite–Sappho and an in-

timacy which is not subjective as necessary for a whitening of sulfur (pp. 178-79). On the rising of Aphrodite connected to the experience of the initiates at Eleusis, see Jung and Kerényi, p. 151.

34. Such attention to the psychic significance of her diet speaks to the distinction, so important to an archetypal psychology, between the concrete and the literal and how this relates to the psychologizing effect of ritual. See Hillman, *Re-Visioning Psychology*, p. 137; *Dream and the Underworld*, pp. 171-74.

35. See Chernin, p. 17, on how following, taking in, the desire for food entails an aesthetic perception: "I noted that the permission to eat was closely linked to a delight in life, a sense of joy and abundance, an awareness of some unexpected meaning or beauty."

36. Hillman, *Re-Visioning Psychology*, p. 146.

37. See Chernin's discussion of the "reenactment of the ritual feast" in Margaret Atwood's *Edible Woman*, in which the main character Marian transcends the "futile symbolism" of anorexia, transforming it to an "expressive symbolism of ritual" (p. 71).

38. In the recent article on anorexia in *Life Magazine* (February 1982), there is a description of the anorexic baking a casserole for her family and being so overcome by its beauty that she runs for a camera. The mother's response: "You don't take a picture of the food, you eat it" (p. 70). But we see: food is aesthetic as we eat it. The entire article basically is a discussion of suppressing, "curing," fixing the demons of the pathology without much entry into the recesses of the patient's psyche. She is left, at the end, looking like a pollyanna child dressed in the "most feminine dress" the family could find in the store, the suppressed sulfuric potencies still emerging through her demands for academic perfectionism, caretaking of parents, supermarket visits at 2:30 a.m., and obsessions around the scale, her "magic" (p. 76). The last therapist (Steven Levenkron) carries the potent forces in a way which allows the patient some distance from her "demon," and takes it off food somewhat, but active imaginal work would have to be done for the "possession" (the identification with the sulfuric element) not to take other literally destructive forms.

39. See Friedrich's discussion of the difficulties of the inherent opposition of Aphrodite and Demeter, pp. 181-91. Also see Jung's alchemical reference to the Virgin Mary, as a feminine Mercurius, who is made pregnant by a seed derived from a "sulphureous fire" (*CW* 12, §470).

40. Hillman, *Re-Visioning Psychology*, p. 9. Also see Rich, "Power & Danger: Works of a Common Woman," in *On Lies, Secrets, and Silence*, particularly p. 257.

Index